World Health Organization
Regional Office for Europe
Copenhagen

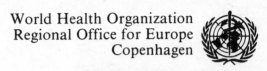

Self-help and health in Europe

New approaches in health care

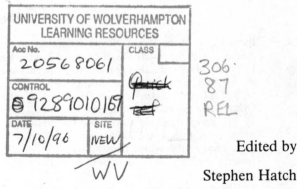

Edited by

Stephen Hatch
Policy Studies Institute
London

and

Ilona Kickbusch
WHO Regional Office for Europe
Copenhagen

ISBN 92 890 1016 9

PRINTED IN DENMARK

CONTENTS

IV   TOWARDS SUPPORTIVE POLICY

The Contributors

Arno van der Avort and Pieter van Harberden work at Tilburg University in The Netherlands.

Bert Bakker and Mathieu Karel were until recently graduate students in the Department of Andragology of the University of Amsterdam.

Arpad Barath is a psychologist in the School of Public Health in Zagreb.

Jan Branckaerts is a member of the Division for Medical Sociology in the Catholic University of Leuven in Belgium.

Mimi Bremer Schulte works in the Faculty of Medicine at the University of Limburg in The Netherlands.

Kurt Buchinger is a member of the Institute for Depth Psychology and Psychotherapy of the University of Vienna.

Alec Dakin and Jennifer Milligan are members of a patients' association in Bristol, England.

Madeline Drake is a freelance researcher in London.

Anders Grimsmo, Gro Helgesen and Christian Borchgrevink belong to the Institute for General Practice of the University of Oslo.

Stephen Hatch is a Senior Research Fellow at the Policy Studies Institute, London.

Bo Henricson is a general practitioner in Swedish Lapland.

Ellis Huber is a health administrator in Berlin who represents the alternative movement.

Ilona Kickbusch is Regional Officer for Health Education of the WHO in Copenhagen.

Robert Lafaille heads the Self-help Groups Project at Tilburg University.

Michael L. Moeller is Professor of Medical Psychology at the University of Frankfurt, but was until recently at the University of Giessen.

Ann Richardson is a Senior Research Fellow at the Policy Studies Institute, London.

David Robinson is Director of the Institute for Health Studies of the University of Hull, England.

I. Szilard, A. Ozsvath and J. Tenyi are members of the Institute of Social Medicine of the University of Pecs in Hungary.

Alf Trojan teaches medical sociology and is leader of the Self-help Groups Research Project at the University of Hamburg.

Christiane Viedma is deputy editor of World Health.

Judy Wilson is the worker on the Nottingham Self-Help Groups Project.

INTRODUCTION

A RE-ORIENTATION OF HEALTH CARE?
Ilona Kickbusch and Stephen Hatch

At the beginning of the 1980s it is becoming increasingly clear that health is not just something between doctors and patients: people are not merely consumers of health care, they pursue health and provide health care themselves through a broad range of activities that until recently have escaped the interest of policy makers, professionals and researchers. We are witness to a reorientation in health care provision which might prove as fundamental in the long run as the rise of the medical profession 150 years ago.

The key word that symbolises this development is self-help. It has come to stand for a variety of sometimes conflicting ideological positions and for many types of activity, a theme we will return to later in this introduction and which is reflected clearly in the articles collected in this volume. It points towards both a new organisational type of care, exemplified by the self-help group, and a rediscovery of types of care that have been there all along but have not sprung to our attention, such as the health care provided in the family framework. It embodies both a 'silent' and a 'noisy' revolution: with groups of people coming together to solve their problems in a mutual manner without consciously claiming to bring about change and with proponents very clearly stating their opposition to the health care system.

In this book we have gathered accounts of recent developments from across the spectrum encompassed by the phenomenon of self-help and from as broad a range of European countries as possible. No one country can claim a vanguard position in the development of self-help, no one type of self-help can claim to be the true format: each can learn from the others. And already both within and between countries the proponents of self-help are building networks of support to add impetus to the current reinterpretation of the role of lay people in health.

As part of its response to the Alma Ata declaration 'Health for All by the year 2000', the Regional Office for Europe of the World Health Organization called together a working group on self-help and health which met in Copenhagen in December 1980. This put forward recommendations for supporting the development of self-

1

help. In following up these recommendations the Regional Office for Europe has organised further workshops and established an Information Centre on Research into Self-help and Health for the European Region (currently situated in Hamburg, Federal Republic of Germany). It has also encouraged self-help initiatives in the European Region through financial support of meetings and publications and has brought together the contributions in this book to document the self-help phenomenon.

The pace at which self-help groups and organisations have come into being over the last ten years has made self-help an issue of continuing debate in both the political and the professional field, leading not only to critical assessment of the quality and efficiency of the health care system in general, but also to hopes of having found a solution to its financial crisis. While self-help activists are discussing a widening of options in health, professionals tend to see self-help as a system supplementary to medical care provision - even as part of its referral system - with physicians defining the extent and content of this care and evaluating its success.

Here lies the root of one of the crucial misunderstandings of the self-help phenomenon: to see and analyse it mainly in its relation to the medical system of health care provision, thus generating a perspective which remains subject to a medical view of health. What has not been stressed with due insistence is the fact that when speaking about self-help, we are concerned with a social and not a medical phenomenon and our analysis must encompass the role of self-help within a totality of social resources applied to health. Given this premise, we enter a new type of debate that opens up perspectives for fundamental changes in care provision as a whole - within both the lay and the medical system - and widens our thinking out towards a social concept of health. It is in this direction that the WHO Regional Office for Europe has oriented its efforts, based on a commitment to the involvement and participation of the community and its members.

What does a social model of health imply?
- it sees the limitations of professional constructions of health and illness and aims to link health behaviours and health decisions with the social content of everyday life;
- it is realistic about the fact that for many people health is not the highest goal in life, and that therefore conceptions of risk-taking must be reconsidered in the light of the values held by and the options available to individuals;
- it sees self-reliance as an expression of human dignity and development;
- it acknowledges that there is more than just one form of curing and healing in every society and that the dominant forms do not necessarily reflect the best solutions;

- it aims at an holistic view of health that integrates the role of social support and human caring into both health maintenance and coping with illness or chronic disease.

Most of these notions are expressed in one way or another by individuals and groups involved in self-help. They question medical definitions of health and illness and the stigma attached to many conditions (for example, alcoholism, obesity or cancer), they want to reclaim areas of normal life which have been defined as medical (for example, pregnancy), they argue for an holistic approach to health problems (patients want to be treated as whole persons, not as the kidney in room 202) and claim decision rights for patients (for example, the choice of treatment) so as to widen their options. But they are also expressing the need for new social forms of care that should be provided for within the 'natural' system of helping.

Ideas put forward by self-help advocates and activists stem in part from more theoretical reappraisals of the role of medicine, such as those put forward by Thomas McKeown, Rene Dubos and Ivan Illich. These stress the overrating of medicine's contribution to health, arguing that environmental and social change and improvements in living conditions have had a far larger impact on the health of populations than medical services. Illich goes even further, and is in agreement with the more radical self-help groups, in stating that medicine can be harmful to patients on account of its iatrogenic effects. Finally, a large literature on holistic health, alternative medicine and new perspectives in healing has evolved over the last ten years, making a strong plea for an ecological model of health that incorporates both a holistic view of a person's interaction with the environment (both physical and social) and the interplay of physical, mental and spiritual health at the individual level. This development partly runs parallel to the self-help movement, partly interacts with it both ideologically and in practice.

Both the professional and the lay system of care have undergone major changes over the last century. Social networks and social structures have been partially destroyed in highly industrialised countries and even though the family, neighbours and friends still provide many basic forms of health care, a wide range of health and social care provision has been medicalised and professionalised. This implies that the possibilities of social learning with regard to certain health conditions, self-care treatments and knowledge have been reduced. At the same time, the illness spectrum in industrialised societies has moved towards chronic diseases, with the result that better ways have to be found for coping with chronic conditions - such as mastectomy - in everyday life.

New social forms in health, such as self-help, develop not only in reaction to dissatisfaction with the medical system, but as a creative response inside the social system to problems that family or friendship networks do not and cannot provide for. With self-help we are therefore witnessing new forms of social learning and coping that might best be analysed in the context of social support and social network research rather than medical sociology or health care provision research. The new groups fulfill social needs for support and the exchange of knowledge - they are a way of 'renewing the social fabric'. Much less has been written about this aspect of social care and support in self-help than about its relation to the professional care givers. Further to this, these new resources in health care can provide support to others: the care burden placed on family members, partricularly the female members, can be eased if patients learn in groups to become more self-reliant and gain new confidence or self-esteem: family members can be helped by discussion of their own problems with caring (for example, groups for family members of alcoholics, parents of disabled children) and knowledge that used to be passed on in a social context can be reactivated, for example, breast feeding, giving birth, first aid.

With these interrelationships in mind, the health education programme of the WHO Regional Office has based its work on the following terminology related to the lay health care system:

- <u>lay care</u> refers to all health care given by lay people to each other in both natural and organised settings and by individuals to themselves; lay care is often referred to as non-professional care, but this term links the phenomenon of lay care too closely to the development of professional services. It goes without saying that the word 'lay' is not used in this context in a derogatory sense, but to convey the recognition that there are major areas of competence in health in the world outside the professional health care system. Until recently, the lay health care resource was greatly under-estimated - estimates of the proportion of all health care that is provided by lay people now range from 60 to 90 per cent (Idler and Levin, 1981). The term 'informal health system' is sometimes used to refer to lay health activities, but for our use this term implies too readily that lay health care is unorganised and without formal structure. This is, of course, not the case as the analysis of family structures or organised self-help reveals.

- <u>self-care</u> refers to unorganised health activities and health-related decision-making by individuals, families, neighbours, friends, colleagues at work, etc.; it encompasses self-medication, self-treatment, social support in illness, first aid in a 'natural setting', i.e. the normal social context of peoples everyday lives. Self-care is definitely the primary health resource in the health care system. The most important feature distinguishing it from self-help is that it does not imply purposeful organisation and is often provided on an ad-hoc basis in intimate settings.

Introduction

- <u>volunteer care</u> denotes forms of lay help that are provided by community members but are organised by agencies such as the church, voluntary associations, charities, etc., which usually have a long tradition in help and care giving. In some European countries the voluntary care system is strongly linked to state services on the basis of 'subsidiarity', in others it is more independent and flexible. Volunteer care differs from new forms of alternative care in its attitude towards change, notwithstanding the fact that links between 'old' and 'new' types of volunteer care have been developing.
- <u>self-help</u> refers to formally or purposefully organised groups in health care, i.e. 'created social units' that find a common - if broad - denominator in a move towards new social forms of coping, lay autonomy and the humanisation of health care. It encompasses both <u>self-help groups</u>, <u>self-help organisations</u> and <u>alternative care</u>, all of which are part of what as a phenomenon has been referred to as the <u>Self-Help Movement</u>. The term 'self-help' is more widely used than 'mutual aid', but the latter may be preferred because it connotes mutuality rather than self-interest.
- <u>self-help groups</u>. - The most widely used definition of self-help groups has been put forward by Katz and Bender (1976) and must be repeated here:

'self-help groups are voluntary, small group structures for mutual aid and the accomplishment of a special purpose. They are usually formed by peers who have come together for mutual assistance in satisfying a common need, overcoming a common handicap or life-disrupting problem, and bringing about desired social and/or personal change. The initiators and members of such groups perceive that their needs are not, or cannot be, met by or through existing social institutions. Self-help groups emphasise face to face social interactions and the assumption of personal responsibility by members. They often provide material assistance, as well as emotional support; they are frequently 'cause'-oriented, and promulgate an ideology or values through which members may attain an enhanced sense of personal identity'.
A simpler and broader definition is 'groups of people who feel they have a common problem and have joined together to do something about it' (Richardson and Goodman, 1983).
To distinguish self-help groups from other interest groups, Katz and Bender introduce the important notion that they start from a condition of powerlessness which they hope to overcome, both inside the social system and towards the medical care system. Women's groups will, for example, 'question their role as care givers in the family and express opposition to the ways they are treated in the medical system.

- <u>alternative services</u>. These services have often developed in the context of self-help groups and/or self-help organisations such as the women's health movement when the principle of mutual aid is extended to alternative service provision, i.e. services not available to certain groups (houses for battered women) or services that promote other forms of treatment or care than those offered by the official health care system. The definition of what constitutes an 'alternative' service will depend on the circumstances of the individual country: it might in some cases be a return to traditional practices, in others promoting new treatments.
- <u>self-help support systems</u>. This term refers to organised support systems for self-help groups, in particular to self-help clearing houses or centres, health shops and health centres that have sprung up in the European Region. They constitute a more or less formalised structure but do not necessarily employ paid staff. Their main functions lie in: networking self-help groups and initiatives, providing resources such as rooms, telephones, organisational help, speaking on behalf of a network of groups, initiating groups and the like.
- <u>self-help organisations/self-help pressure groups</u>. These organisations, which can vary enormously in scope and size, organise around a general or specific issue in health care organisation (for example, natural childbirth), health promotion (for example, womens health groups), disease prevention (for example, ecological issues) to bring about changes in the health system or society at large. They focus on creating pressure towards change and often they represent the most visible, action-oriented part of self-help, trying even in their larger structures to adhere to principles of self-organisation and mutuality. Self-help organisations may run specialist self-help groups (such as La Leche League) or they may be a 'generalist' association of self-help groups (such as the Deutsche Arbeitsgemeinschaft Selbsthilfegruppen).

This variety of lay health care can be placed along a self-help continuum which ranges from individual involvement in self-care to possibly large scale action on the part of self-help organisations. This range has been most adequately reflected in the women's health movement in claiming a woman's right to her own body. Women had realised in consciousness raising groups that many aspects of their lives were defined and controlled by medicine, that medical and scientific knowledge that was allegedly value free contributed to maintain their dependence. This theoretical critique of medicine (based on women's experiences in the health care system) led in practice to self-help groups, advice centres and self-help clinics. The most prominent project to come out of this movement was the women's self-help manual, <u>Our Bodies</u>

<u>Ourselves</u>, which by now has been translated into several languages and can be seen as a milestone and starting point for many self-help activities all over the world. Many of the radical ideas of this movement have filtered into other self-help groups through reports in the mass media and have now become commonly accepted by the self-help movement in general: to see the idea of self-reliance as basically possible, to give back to people the confidence in their own knowledge and skills, to let people trust their own experiences and to convince them that they can help themselves and each other.

The self-help continuum makes it necessary to clarify what part of self-help and lay care we are speaking about when we devise health care policies - a point which we will take up in the conclusions to this book. We hope that our selection of articles helps reflect the broad variety of forms of care giving in the lay system.

The four contributions that comprise Part I examine the phenomenon of self-help and self-care from different perspectives: Robinson argues that self-help is an important component of primary health care; Dean provides an authoritative review of self-care; Richardson looks at self-help as a group activity and Trojan considers self-help as a movement, comparing France with the Federal Republic of Germany. It becomes clear that self-help groups can occupy at least three positions in relation to the health care system: they can function within the system, work next to the system or express clear opposition to formal medicine (Kickbusch, 1979).

Self-help also poses both opportunities and challenges to the medical professions. The contributions to Part II are all by professionals sympathetic to self-help. Buchinger considers the contribution of self-help to psychotherapy; Moeller, who has made a major contribution to the development of self-help in the Federal Republic of Germany, argues for a sympathetic response by medical practitioners; Bremer-Schulte shows how self-help has been given an important place in the medical curriculum of the University of Limburg; Henricson describes how he has encouraged self-care as a general practitioner in his own rather unusual context; and Branckaerts describes the explorations of a social scientist in the field of self-help.

This section shows that there already exists a substantial 'grey zone' between self-help activities and professional care in which lay people and professionals can collaborate on terms of greater equality. To our minds it denotes a new stage in the development of self-help in Europe.

The diversity of the self-help phenomenon is further emphasised by the ten contributions to Part III which provide examples of actual groups. Selection for this chapter proved the most difficult. There are mutual aid groups for nearly every disease category listed by WHO, as well as groups for a wide variety of psycho-social problems: parents without partners, parents of terminally ill children, Emotions Anonymous, to name but a few. Further, our examples were intended to testify the variety of expression self-help can take in different cultures and different types of health system. These contributions again exemplify the varying roles of professionals in relation to lay participants, and the wide typology of groups ranging from a search for empowerment to a systematic model of self-control.

Part IV considers the place of self-help in the health care system and the kinds of support it needs. Lafaille sees the organisations of lay people as a new tier in the structure of health care; Bakker and Karel warn against co-opting self-help; and proposals for suporting self-help come from a workshop held at Hohr-Grenzhausen under the auspices of WHO. Finally, we attempt to distil some of the policy implications of the development of self-help in the 1970s. This development is part of a larger pattern of change. In the Federal Republic of Germany, perhaps more than elsewhere, self-help has been explicitly part of a challenge to accepted institutions and patterns of authority and closely linked to the alternative and ecology movement. But everywhere it embodies some new thinking abut the roles of lay people, professionals and the state. In the less favourable economic circumstances of the 1980s, self-help could be a part of an alibi for a deterioration in the standards and coverage of official provision for health care. More optimistically, these circumstances offer a stimulus to build on the reappraisal of medicine and health that marked the 1970s, and to find ways of recognising and supporting self-help as an integral social component of health care.

This leads back to the original conceptual statement made in this introduction: when speaking of new social resources and forms of health care we must see that they are related not only to changes and challenges with respect to the professional care system but also to developments in 'natural' systems of helping. On a most basic level we are searching for a new ecology of caring in society.

References

Boston Women's Health Collective (1978), Our Bodies Ourselves, Allen Lane, London.

Katz, A.H. and Bender, E. (1976) The Strength in Us: self-help groups in the modern world, Franklin Watts, New York.

Kickbusch, Ilona (1980) 'Medizinische Selbsthilfegruppen', Jahrbuch fur Kritische Medizin, Band 5, Berlin.

Levin, L.S. and Idler, E.L. (1981) The Hidden Health Care System: mediating structures and medicine, Ballinger, Cambridge, Mass.

Introduction

Richardson, Ann and Goodman, Meg (1983) <u>Self-help and Social Care: mutual aid organisations in practice</u>, Policy Studies Institute, London.

PART 1 THE SELF-HELP PHENOMENON

SELF-HELP GROUPS IN PRIMARY HEALTH CARE
David Robinson

Primary health care consists of those basic health measures that should apply to all people, in both developed and developing countries. The Declaration of Alma-Ata (1978) holds that primary health care addresses the main health problems in the community, providing promotive, preventive, curative and rehabilitative services. As such it

> ... includes at least: education concerning prevailing health problems and the methods of preventing and controlling them; promotion of food supply and proper nutrition; an adequate supply of safe water and basic sanitation; maternal and child health care, including family planning; immunization against the major infectious diseases; prevention and control of locally endemic diseases; appropriate treatment of common diseases and injuries; and provision of essential drugs ...

In developing countries, adequate primary health care may require the provision of services where none exist, and in developed countries, the refocusing of existing services and a reordering of priorities. In all countries it requires the formulation and implementation of programmes for health development that include, among other considerations, the assumption that there will be substantial community participation.

Community participation

One of the major obstacles to the development of adequate primary health care in the past has been the paucity of clear thinking about the kind of health workers needed to provide the necessary services at the local level. Where it has become recognised that most preventive measures and a large proportion of promotive and curative procedures do not need extensive professional training, there has been a move toward recruiting primary health workers from the local population (Djukanovic and Mach, 1975). This is a crucial step in implementing a primary health care philosophy that acknowledges that '... any significant improvement in the physical, mental and social wellbeing to a large extent will depend on the individual's and the community's will to fend for themselves ...' (Mahler, 1977).

Fending for oneself means ensuring that any programme of primary health care can be implemented 'at a cost that the community can afford to maintain at every stage of their development in the spirit of self-reliance and self-determination' (The Declaration of Alma-Ata, 1978). This should not be seen, however, as a cheap substitute for having available a well-developed technology and properly trained manpower. But in all countries, developed or developing, the use of specialist equipment, human or mechanical, must be determined by the part it can play in raising the overall health standards of the community, as opposed to undermining it by expropriating too high a proportion of available health resources.

Fending for oneself also means that all citizens have a duty to create the conditions and contribute to the measures by which everyone can live a healthy life. Developed countries no less than developing ones must learn to fend for themselves in this sense.

Once primary health care is equated with the creation and maintenance of a sound and dignified life for everyone, the importance of citizen involvement becomes clear. No one is exempt, since at the local level everyone has something to contribute, be it technical expertise or manual labour to aid in building a neighbourhood waste-disposal system, an understanding of contraception or nutrition, having the time to care for young children whose parents are at work, or meeting with others to solve some common health problem in a self-help group.

Self-help groups
Medicine as practiced by the medical establishment of developed countries has begun to be questioned and criticised by some people. There are those who even regard it as a threat to health, not merely in the technical sense of malpractice, clinical iatrogenesis, and inappropriate treatment, but in the wider political sense of diverting attention from the social-structural and environmental causes of ill health. Not surprisingly, there is growing hostility towards any professional and physician-based health care system that undermines the power of the individual to heal himself or shape his own environment. Moreover, there has been a rapid and substantial growth in self-help groups and projects that, taken together, now represent a significant feature of contemporary life.

Considerable attention has been given to self-help by professionals and governments as well as by interested laymen and the media. There is hardly any wide-circulation magazine or professional article that has not carried an article on some 'health by the people' project or on the activities of some particular self-help group. Several WHO publications have set out the philosophy, organisation and achievements of alternative approaches to meeting the basic health needs of developing countries (Djukanovic and Mach, 1975; Newell, 1975).

It is often claimed that in many societies the natural support systems, such as the church, the neighbourhood and the family, are in decline. As a result, there is a search for community by people who feel helpless or hopeless and without control over their own destiny. For many, the world has moved too fast. And it is too big, too indifferent to quality, to individual differences, and to basic human needs.

Self-help is a natural response to this situation, and one manifestation of this is the growth of self-help groups. The self-help group is not just a refuge: it is much more positive. In addition to providing mutual support for those who share a particular problem, it finds practical solutions to specific difficulties and gives members an opportunity to build, on the basis of mutual trust and understanding, a new set of relationships - for some, even, a new way of life.

Some groups, such as Alcoholics Anonymous, are well known and long established. But there are also thousands of newer, less well known groups - for schizophrenics, people with particular skin diseases, smokers, phobics, the anxious, the depressed, gamblers, homosexuals, people with hypertension, people with cancer, child batterers, widows, parents of handicapped children, and many others. Several writers have assembled some of the scattered information on specific groups in developed countries in order to determine what, in practice, self-help groups do (Caplan and Killilea, 1976; Katz and Bender, 1976).

Killilea (1976), for example, has identified certain characteristics of self-help groups. These include:

1. Common experience of members. The care-giver has the same disability as the care-receiver.
2. Mutual help and support. The individual is a member of a group that meets regularly in order to provide mutual aid.
3. The helper principle. In a situation in which people help others with a common problem, it may be the helper who benefits most from the exchange.
4. Differential association. The reinforcement of a self-perception of normality hastens members' abandonment of their previously deviant identities.
5. Collective will-power and belief. Each person looks to others in the group for validation of his feelings and attitudes.
6. Information exchange. The promotion of greater factual understanding of the problem, as opposed to intrapsychic understanding.
7. Constructive action towards shared goals. Groups are action-oriented, their philosophy being that members learn by doing and are changed by doing.

Self-help for what?

The range of problems dealt with by particular self-help groups is immense. In relation to any aspect of physical condition, mental well-being or social situation, there are some people who are 'abnormal'. There are those with illnesses such as cancer, or disablements such as colostomy, stammering, skin blemishes or blindness. There are those with abnormal mental attributes, such as chronic feelings of depression, guilt or fear. There are those whose interpersonal behaviour is abnormal, such as those who batter children, make love to them, or choose not to have them. And there are those with some abnormal personal situation, such as being homeless, or a mental patient, or divorced.

Such 'abnormalities', however, are not necessarily minor problems: the practical difficulties may not be insurmountable. What turns them into major problems is the way they are viewed by those affected or by others. Despite efforts to discount the attitudes of others - for example, by saying 'Society doesn't understand' - it is easy to see how, for many people, the combination of an abnormality plus social stigma assumes central and overwhelming importance.

In developed countries the 'real' problem for most members of self-help groups is that they are 'abnormal' according to the lights of a society geared to high standards of normality and are perhaps 'dependent' in a society that puts great stress on independence. They are made to feel that they have failed, or are inadequate, as people. Not surprisingly, the end result is often a diminished sense of personal worth.

Paradoxically, perhaps, the first step toward getting rid of a problem is to concentrate on it. In self-help groups people focus on one clearly defined problem. In developed countries this may mean that people admit they really are alcoholics, for example, or are overweight. In a rural village in a developing country, it may entail admitting that certain traditional routines or priorities must be questioned, and that an inadequate or non-existent water system, for instance, is really not an acceptable state of affairs. An integral part of this concentration on the problem, whether in an Alcoholics Anonymous group or in a village in Tanzania, is recognition that it has to be solved by us. In both situations outside help, expertise or support may be utilised, but in neither situation can outsiders be expected actually to solve the problem: self-reliance and self-determination at the basic group level are required.

Sharing information and techniques
Once the problem is acknowledged, the second stage of the self-help process can begin: sharing information and techniques. This may be at the level of physical aids, basic engineering, information about official agencies and rights, or anything that makes it easier to handle the technicalities of a shared problem. Clearly, the range of specific practical aids being used in self-help programmes is immense. Similarly, the mechanics of sharing range from village assembly or formal group meetings to informal

meetings of group members, telephone contact networks, correspondence and newsletters, or tape exchanges and radio contacts when the members are geographically dispersed or prevented by their shared problem from meeting face to face. No matter what is being shared, and no matter what the mechanics of sharing, the underlying principle is the same: the dissemination of knowledge, expertise, skills and techniques to those who need to use them in order to solve some common problem.

For example, In Touch, an English self-help group of parents of mentally handicapped children, has a network of correspondence magazines. In these, parents of children with a similar condition contribute to a 'magazine' which consists of letters from each of them. As each mother receives the magazine, she reads all the other letters and replaces her own most recent letter with a new one commenting on the points raised. Each member receives as many as a dozen letters every few weeks while writing only one, and some of the magazines have been circulating for several years.

In clubs for hypertensives in Zagreb, Yugoslavia, members learn to control their own blood pressure. These are described more fully in Barath's contribution to this book, but it is clear from an inspection of club logs that, for the great majority of members, blood pressure declines significantly over the period of attendance at the clubs, and can be maintained at a satisfactory level. In addition, the establishment of the clubs for hypertensives has had important benefits in terms of economy and saving time.

Destigmatisation

There is more to dealing with most health problems than disseminating information and handling practicalities. For some people a major difficulty is not the particular health problem itself, but the fact that they are people with the problem. An important function of many self-help groups, therefore, is to disperse the social discreditability of the shared problem.

One way of destigmatising a problem is by changing the self-perception of those affected, a feat partly achieved by meeting others in the same situation and therefore feeling less 'odd'. 'Self-help groups,' said the Director of the National Council for One Parent Families, '... have a double value to lone parents and their children in providing the mutual support that is so helpful to them and also helping the children to have a real social identity by realising that there are many lone parents and the children are, therefore, not in any way unusual'. In addition, it is common for nearly all self-help groups to direct their destigmatising efforts toward changing those who are seen as the cause of the stigma: 'the general public' or 'society' - or just all those who 'do not understand'. In short, self-help groups aim to destigmatise the problem by changing the attitudes of both their members and outsiders.

15

Self-help as a way of life

Successful self-help groups and projects are much more than meeting-places for people who feel discriminated against or overwhelmed by a common problem or by some aspect of late twentieth-century life. Self-help offers most to people when it manages to combine mutual support for those who share a common problem with activities and projects that encourage personal development and enable people to influence the quality of their everyday lives.

In developing countries, work on particular health projects cannot be considered in isolation from nation-building. Most development projects in Tanzania, for example, contain a self-help element: 'Thus in the construction of a health centre, certain buildings such as kitchens and mortuaries are not usually provided for in the financial estimates; it is expected that they will be built on a self-help basis' (Chagula and Tarimo, 1975). Self-help is a feature of nation-building projects that come under the auspices of other government ministries but have a direct effect on the health of the people. For instance, the Ntomoko project in Tanzania, in which 125 km of water trench was dug on a self-help basis, will greatly improve the health of the people in the 23 villages served by the water pipeline.

The core of the self-help process is to settle, from among all the problems that one faces, on a clear, understandable and manageable one, to manage it, and then to build a new life as a person, group or community able to control everyday problems, and thus one's destiny. Self-help then becomes a way of life.

Self-help and primary health care

The Declaration of Alma-Ata calls on all governments to 'formulate national policies, strategies and plans of action to launch and sustain primary health care as part of a comprehensive national health system ...'. National frameworks for co-ordinated action are, of course, essential. But if any significant impact is to be made on the world's health problems, then primary health care systems must take into account and build on the ideas, activities, priorities and aspirations of the people. In order that national programmes may go forward 'in the spirit of self-reliance and self-determination', the people of all countries, both developed and developing, must be able to 'participate individually and collectively in the planning and implementation of health care'. Self-help groups and projects can provide a basis for such community participation.

A large proportion of the self-help groups in developed countries operate quite independently of the formal health services. In fact, the impetus for the establishment of many groups has been the lack of adequate understanding, care, treatment or support from the various health professions. This

16

immediately raises the question of whether these 'independent' groups can contribute to a coherent and comprehensive primary health care system in anything but a purely ad hoc manner.

Evidence from various parts of the world indicates that health services at the local level do accommodate and respond to the activities of even the most 'independent' of self-help groups when those groups are felt to be providing an important source of primary health care. Alcoholics Anonymous (the Sobriety Society in the USSR), for example, has developed into an international network of groups that co-operate with formal health and social services in an attempt to provide comprehensive care for those with drinking problems, yet Alcoholics Anonymous retains complete control over its own self-help philosophy, group activities and membership.

In contrast to the independent groups, other self-help groups and organisations are very much the brainchildren of health workers who are still closely involved with them. This raises several important questions. To what extent are these groups 'self-help' in the usual meaning of the phrase? What role do the health workers play in the everyday activities of the group? How able are such groups to develop structures and procedures that best suit the needs of their members? What are the implications of being so closely involved with the formal health services - for the group and its members, for the neighbourhoods in which they are situated, and for the development of more satisfactory systems of primary health care?

The clubs for hypertensives in the Tresjevka and Remetinec areas of Zagreb provide a clear illustration of both the disadvantages and advantages of self-help enterprises in which professional health workers are closely involved. The role of the health worker has been to get the clubs started, to organise the election of officers, to train the members in self-monitoring techniques, and to provide guidance and aid. There is no doubt that the clubs are very successful within the strict limits in which they were established. They have gathered people together who can now perfectly adequately monitor and control their blood pressure. But it is also true that, although many new clubs are being formed, many of the older clubs are becoming rather staid and set in their ways; membership is static, the same people have held office in some clubs ever since they began, and the same people tended to measure blood pressure at each meeting. The clubs, although self-governing, are still very much under the guidance of the associated medical staff.

It was one of the original aims of those who established the clubs that patients should be members for only a limited period, a year or eighteen months, after which they would have learned how to control their blood pressure and established a dietary, exercise and relaxation regime that would maintain it at a satisfactory level. But, as the health workers have found out, once people come together and become 'a group' in order to provide mutual support and encouragement to each other, they do not just 'fade away' as soon as 'the problem' has been brought under control.

Fortunately, given the enthusiasm of many club members and the interest and involvement of various health workers, there is the possibility of responding to and building on this situation. Both the members and the associated health workers have ideas about how the clubs for hypertensives might develop into more general health education, care and maintenance groups. One club is keen to develop programmes for diabetics and people with obesity and heart disorders. The members of another club want to set up teams that will make home visits to provide social care for elderly people and the handicapped. The members of a club based in a furniture factory screen their workmates and are beginning to assume basic health education functions in relation to smoking and other issues. A film about abortion, which had been shown at the factory, stimulated discussion about gynaecological problems and was taken by some club members and shown in their local neighbourhood centres.

Once group members have learned the basic skills of controlling their blood pressure - or whatever their 'problem' is - they can be taught more and more health skills and techniques in relation to everyday physical and mental health care. Subgroups of members can develop particular sets of skills and become 'resources' not only for other group members but for their families, neighbours, friends and workmates. In this way, self-help groups, instead of being inward looking and concerned only with the particular problems that brought the members together, can become the ideal medium for the education and development of basic health workers. Self-help group members, because of their own experience, are well placed to understand that there are many technical skills that the general public can easily learn, and that mutual aid and support are essential components in the handling of most modern health problems.

Group members need to be given the opportunity to learn new skills and thus develop into basic health workers for their immediate locality. The groups themselves benefit from contact with each other, which can help them build up a repertoire of knowledge about ways of handling a wide range of health problems. In addition, representatives from the group are in an ideal position to explain the value of self-help groups to health and neighbourhood centres and to workplaces that do not yet have them. Through close links with sympathetic health workers on the one hand and with local neighbourhood organisations on the other, self-help groups have the potential for making a significant contribution to raising the overall health standards of the community. They may be a model for an important new element in a much-needed new approach to health and health care.

References and relevant literature

Caplan, G. and Killilea, M. (eds.) (1976) Support Systems and Mutual Help: multidisciplinary explorations, Grune and Stratton, New York.

Chagula, W.K. and Tarimo, E. (1975) 'Meeting basic health needs in Tanzania' in K.W. Newell (ed.), Health by the People, WHO, Geneva.

Declaration of Alma Ata (1978) in Primary Health Care: Alma Ata 1978, World Health Organisation, Geneva.

Djukanovic, V. and Mach, E.P. (eds) (1975) Alternative Approaches to Meeting Basic Health Needs in Developing Countries: A Joint UNICEF/WHO Study, World Health Organisation, Geneva.

Katz, A. and Bender, E.I. (eds.) (1976) The Strength in Us: self-help groups in the modern world, Franklin Watts, New York.

Killilea, M. (1976) 'Mutual Help Organisations: interpretations in the literature' in Caplan and Killilea op.cit..

Mahler, H. (1977) 'Problems of Medical Affluence', WHO Chronicle, 31, 8.

Newell, K.W. (ed.) (1975) Health by the People, WHO, Geneva.

Robinson,D. and Henry, S. (1977) Self-help and health: mutual aid for modern problems, Martin Robertson, London.

Note: An earlier version of this article appeared in Social Science and Medicine, Vol. 14A, 1980.

SELF-CARE: WHAT PEOPLE DO FOR THEMSELVES
Kay Dean

Self-care is the individual health behaviour component of self-help.
It is the primary health behaviour which shapes the type and
amount of professional services utilised by the population. As such
self-care has perhaps been the subject which has generated the
greatest amount of debate among professionals, social scientists
and policy analysts. Disagreement has generally focused on two
major areas of concern:
1. the importance of the health maintenance activities of
    individuals in shaping health;
2. the competence of individuals and families for the treatment
    of illness.
Discussions centred on both topics tend to polarise self-care
and professional care. Self-care is generally seen as a recent
development, either as a reaction to the dysfunctional effects of
industrial societies and their technically dominated health services
systems (Levin et al, 1976), or as a potential area of care where
responsibility can be given, primarily for the treatment of minor
illnesses, by overburdened physicians to patients and their families.
(Levin et al, 1976; Williamson and Danaher, 1978). These
conceptualisations of self-care are manifestations of an implicit
assumption that the major form of health care is medical care.
Suggestions by physicians that more care can be turned over to lay
people than has previously occurred or been thought desirable
(Levin et al, 1976, p.33), imply that it is the medical system that
determines self-care practice rather than vice-versa.
Self-care is neither a new nor a fringe phenomenon. It is the
basic health behaviour in all societies. The renewed controversy
regarding the subject is undoubtedly a reaction to dysfunctional
effects of contemporary health services systems. However, the
current issues of access to professional care and the dangers of
caustic medicines and unproven treatment procedures as well as
concern regarding cost, benefit and profit are similar to the major
issues surrounding self-care developments in the 17th and 18th
centuries (Risse et al, 1977). What is new is the growing official,
scientific and professional recognition of the vital role of the
individual in the maintenance of health and the treatment of
illness.

Health maintenance by individuals

Statistical evidence accumulated in recent times has documented the primacy of the environment in shaping the general health of populations (McKeown, 1976; McKinlay and McKinlay, 1977). Public and personal sanitation, housing and general living conditions, and especially host-resistance to disease arising from adequate food supplies are important factors combating disease in social settings where infectious diseases are the major threats to life. In situations of insufficient supply of nutrients there is little that individuals can do to maintain health. However, except under the most deprived conditions, informed behaviour can facilitate the conservation and consolidation of what limited health resources are available to the individual.

In highly developed industrialised societies, the health maintenance activities of individuals assume a more basic role in shaping the general health structure of the population (Belloc, 1972; Carlsen et al, 1971). Diseases of life style and chronic disorders of ageing are the major health problems of affluent societies. This does not mean that the impact of the environment on health is diminished in affluent societies. Expanding potential for individuals to protect and improve their health is paralleled by increasing environmental threats in the form of polluted air and water supplies, food additives and the development of chemically-resistant micro-organisms. Furthermore, the increasing dangers are not limited to the physical environment. The social environment is now known to play a decisive role in the capacity of the individual to combat disease. The vulnerability of the human organism to disease agents is affected by the stress experience of the individual. The most recent evidence indicates that morbidity experience is not a direct function of stress, but that the impact of stress is filtered through mediating structures of social support (Levin and Idler, 1981). Paradoxically, some threats to the coping capacity of individuals arise from many 'advances' in developed societies. These may range from counterproductive technological development to institutional 'solutions' to social problems which weaken the social supports and resources available to individuals.

The organism's capacity for adaption in order to maintain equilibrium is an essential element in the maintenance of health. Thus the rate of changing circumstances which must be assimilated and the disintegration of mediating forces which support human adaption are, along with dangers in the physical environment and those in many occupational settings, major threats to health and well-being in advanced industrial societies. Health knowledge and the caring capacities of lay persons thus become directly related to disease prevention and the maintenance of existing levels of health and functional capacity.

Mutual aid groups have become an important resource for persons with problems for which medical services do not provide effective solutions. Individuals learn about their specific problems, methods for coping with and/or solving and sharing the problem. The psychological and social support provided during the learning process creates an environment favourable for the effective application of treatment behaviour and coping skills.

In spite of the growing body of evidence regarding the complexity of interacting factors contributing to disease, policies related to health and health services are still predominantly based on the traditional medical model and on single factor theories of etiology. Illness continues to be widely perceived as an external invader which damages a previously healthy body. Prevention and social medicine receive low priority in medical research and in the development of health systems. The health maintenance and treatment activities of individuals and mutual aid groups are even less valued and developed. Habits of daily living, methods of coping with stress, mutual aid, informed participation in efforts to protect the environment and other forms of self-care/self-help may be major determinants of health in developed societies. As suggested by Levin et al, investments in lay health resources may be more progressive than those excessively concentrated in curative medical services.

> Skills possessed (by the lay population) are immediately available as productive output, self-adjusting and discriminatingly applied according to self-observed effectiveness. Self-care skills can accrue, become assimilated as coping skills, and passed on to others through the process of socialisation. Thus, over time, self-care skills can have a multiplier effect. (Levin et al, 1976, p.26)

Competence of individuals and families for the treatment of illness
Discussions regarding the competence of lay persons for the treatment of illness have generally ignored the fact that most illness is treated by the ill person with or without the aid of family members. Physicians have until recently considered self-care as dangerous and/or as causing potentially serious delay in seeking medical care. Thus the subject was considered in terms of methods to avoid or change self-care practices. This professional perspective reflects an attitude that medical care is the major form of health care while the opposite situation is the reality. Professional consultation for the symptoms of illness is the supplementary and peripheral form of illness behaviour.

Once illness is experienced, all interactions with medical systems arise from lay evaluations of symptoms. If a symptom is not considered serious, it may be ignored or observed for a period of time. If treatment is considered necessary then self-treatment or a professional contact will be chosen. When a decision is made for professional consultation, participation in treatment, once the contact is made, will also depend on decisions of the individual. The majority of symptoms are never presented for medical treatment. No form of medical system could respond to the volume of demand if they were. Furthermore, decisions to consult doctors differ significantly among persons experiencing the same illnesses, and many consultations are for symptoms for which most people never seek care.

That is not to say that the professional perspective has not affected the lay population. An escalating tendency over the past several decades to medicalise both social problems and normal physiological functions and changes has created unrealistic expectations among lay persons regarding the function and potential of medical services. The coping skills of individuals and appropriate use of social resources are not enhanced by these developments. The disease related workload of general practice has been estimated to include patients with serious illnesses in only 15 per cent of the cases, while about 65 per cent of the consultations are for minor illnesses and 20 per cent for chronic conditions (Anderson et al, 1977). One investigation of the content of general practice discovered that 20 per cent of the consultations were related to social problems rather than to disease. Furthermore, in those consultations which were for physical symptoms, no firm diagnosis could be established in 43 per cent of the cases (Risse et al, 1977).

In an investigation of patterns of medical consultation in a Danish county, 235 out of 304 general practitioners registered consultations during office hours for one working day (Aarhus, 1979). Fifty-two per cent of the 9,228 contacts were office visits, while 40 per cent were telephone contacts and seven per cent home visits. For 13 per cent of the consulations, no illness was found. An additional four per cent of the contacts were for problems related to alcohol or other chemical addiction, marriage, economic or other types of difficulties and nervous complaints not appropriate for the psychiatric classifications. A final three per cent of the conditions could not be included in diagnostic or body system classifications. No estimates were given regarding the proportions of the 9,292 illness related contacts which were life-threatening or disabling conditions as compared with non-serious, self-limiting or trivial conditions.

The medicalisation of normal bodily functions and life changes such as menstruation, pregnancy, menopause and ageing implies that physiological variations and sensations (especially uncomfortable ones) are illnesses. A possible consequence of this development is to increase the incidence of discomfort related to these physiological variations. A related danger is the possibility of negative effects on adaption to physical and functional alterations in advanced stages of the life cycle. For example, negative stereotypes and low expectations play an important role in a cycle of reduced functioning among elderly persons.

Professionals in the field of mental health have postulated that a person's degree of defensiveness towards ageing may be an important predictor of psychological adaptability in later life (Fiske, 1980; Gaity and Vamer, 1980). Yet cultural stereotypes, professional providers of care and even much of the literature on ageing underestimate the functional capacity of older people. Their psychological and social problems are often defined as illness (Birren and Renner, 1980; WHO, 1980). Depression which increases with age is an especially important symptom to consider in this regard. The term is often misapplied when a situation of unhappiness is confused with a specific clinical diagnostic category (Arie, 1977; Fiske, 1980). Accelerated losses and changes of later life result quite naturally in reduced morale and normal depression. The habits of stress reduction practised by individuals throughout life may be decisive factors in effective coping with the inevitable changes of old age. Yet little is known about patterns of stress reduction in general populations.

This brief discussion of self-care suggests the importance of building a body of knowledge, regarding the range of self-care and mutual aid practices in general populations and the factors shaping alternative patterns of self-care behaviour. Some information is available on the subject.

Self-care research

Past research interest in self-care has been predominantly concerned with health maintenance components of individual behaviour or with the utilisation of preventive health services (Becker, 1974; Belloc, 1972; Breslow and Engstrom, 1980). In most research investigations of behavioural responses to illness, the focus has been on the utilisation of physician and hospital services (McKinlay, 1972), delay in seeking care (Battistella, 1971) and patient compliance with medical regimes (Davis, 1966; Marston, 1970). Centred in a professional view of illness, lay persons in these studies were defined as recipients of professional care. Self-evaluation of symptoms and active self-care were ignored. The ill person's participation in treatment consisted of passive compliance with medical directives. Non-compliance, however extensive, was deviant behaviour, the source of which was sought in some negative characteristic of the patient. In one unusual exception when consultation behaviour was investigated from a patient perspective, it was found that patients actively evaluate and choose among professional directives based on their own experience and lay consultation (Stimson, 1974).

Paralleling the growing patient activism of recent years and the recognition of the limits of medical care, there has been some shift in research focus towards the study of self-medication, the role of the family in health care, and the range of self-care practised by individuals as the first level of care. The value of the available information is predominantly descriptive. Very few conclusions or generalisations are possible. However, while still quite limited, the findings of these studies document the basic role of self-care. Self-evaluation of symptoms and lay decisions regarding self-treatment, professional treatment or a combination of the two are the predominant forms of health care in illness (Dean, 1981).

Consultation with other lay persons is known to be an important component of the decision-making process regarding behavioural responses to illness. Lay referral is an especially important factor in decisions regarding professional consultation. Treatment responses to symptoms may be of a purely ameliorative character or they may be a type of secondary prevention directed toward the source of the problem. Age appears to be an important factor in the type of treatment responses to illness (Dean, 1980). Self-medication is extensive, increases with age, is more frequent among women and often takes place with drugs already in the home, frequently prescription drugs obtained for an earlier illness episode (Carlsen et al, 1971; Dunnel and Cartwright, 1972; Knapp and Knapp, 1972; Rabin and Bush, 1975).

Few studies have attempted to evaluate self-treatment, but those which have report the treatment practices to be predominantly appropriate and effective (Anderson et al, 1977; Pedersen, 1976). Yet there is evidence that health knowledge and basic treatment skills are poor, especially among elderly persons (Litman, 1971). The findings from one investigation suggest that self-treatment may approximate professional treatment of the same condition, but in a less intense form of therapy, for example, weaker medications (Gannik and Jespersen, 1980).

While some basic data are available regarding the extent of self-care, little is known about the range, process and appropriateness of self-treatment, nor about the factors which are more important in shaping self-care responses to illness. The information available is seriously limited in scope and methodology, restricting its usefulness in contributing to the establishment of a data base of knowledge regarding self-care.

This is partially due to the fact that many of the investigations which contain relevant information were designed for purposes other than the study of self-care behaviour. They are often limited to descriptive information comparing non-prescription drug use with the use of prescription drugs. Even this simple information is compounded by incompatibilities in definitions of prescription drugs. For example, non-prescription drugs suggested by doctors have sometimes been classified as prescription medications, while prescription medicines taken as directed by physicians have been labelled as self-decisions. Additionally, drug prescription requirements differ significantly among countries.

25

Consulting behaviour is another area of conceptual confusion in investigations of self-care response to illness. Self-care behaviour is often defined as a substitute behaviour for professional consultation resulting in polarisation of the two concepts. Some investigators, however, conceptualise self-care as a continuum of responses to illness in which professional consultation is one option which may or may not result from the self-evaluation of symptoms.

One type of response to illness has been almost totally neglected. There is often an implicit assumption that symptoms should be treated. Therefore, decisions to do nothing about symptoms are rarely given equal consideration with other types of behavioural responses in the analysis of data.

Perhaps the most serious methodological limitations of the available self-care data are related to sampling procedures. Many investigations were conducted on convenience samples, often patient groups. The findings of these studies are of questionable value if the sample size is small. When self-care responses to illness are investigated in samples of patients, behaviour which is not associated with the use of professional services may be overlooked. Information on the self-care behaviour of people who seldom or never consult physicians is excluded.

Those studies which are limited to other sub-groups of general populations such as persons on low incomes, urban populations or families with small children preclude analyses of the effects of membership in the particular sub-group. Comparisons between investigations also become more difficult. In order to establish a data base of knowledge regarding self-care it is necessary to collect data using random sampling procedures from general population samples of sufficient size to analyse the factors shaping the responses in sub-groups of the population. The research instruments used in these investigations need to be standardised, especially the definitions of self-care variables in order to facilitate replication studies and comparative analyses of data from different populations. In the establishment of this data base, special attention should be given to an area about which nothing is known. That is, the extent to which self-care is directed toward disabling and life-threatening diseases.

Independent variable analyses

The most consistent differences in behavioural responses to illness appear to be related to the sex of the respondents. The virtually unvarying tendency for women to use medications more often than men is particularly significant. Very little is known about the factors shaping medication behaviour in women, or about the factors contributing to sex differences in morbidity experience and the utilisation of professional services. It appears that life situational differences, especially those related to social network and social support are important factors in this regard.

26

Investigations focussed on behavioural difficulties among women seem necessary to identify and determine the relative importance of factors shaping female health behaviour.

Situational difficulties in the availability of social support are also important factors to consider in the self-care behaviour of older people. The impact of cultural stereotypes, reduced expectations and possible differences in professional treatment of older people in relation to younger persons are equally important to consider.

The influence of social network as a variable shaping self-care behaviour extends beyond traditional considerations of lay referral. The role of social support in stress reduction and provision of care and information should be considered in relation to self-care patterns in both health and illness behaviour (Levin and Idler, 1981). Family health behaviour and functioning are especially relevant in this regard. There is evidence that a tendency to rely on doctors for counsel on non-medical life problems is related to both the use of medications and physician consultation for minor illnesses (Dean, 1980). Investigations of the relationships between various forms of social support and the forces shaping reliant attitudes towards physicians are needed. The impact of mutual aid groups on individual self-care behaviour has been a totally neglected area of research.

Extensive data have been collected on the effects of occupational, income and social class differences on utilisation of professional services. Little is known, however, about possible situational constraints on sick role behaviour due to these variables. For example, there is evidence that bed rest when ill as opposed to the maintenance of normal routines may depend on such situational differences (Dean, 1980).

An additional area about which little is known is the role and importance of information in shaping self-care patterns. Information was found to be more important in the use of coping and development services than self-rated health, the presence of a chronic health problem and functional health (Gruder, 1980). Awareness of the existence and functions of various service agencies was the dominant factor in explaining their use. However, awareness of ancillary services was found to decrease with age, an important finding in view of the relative needs of older people.

The efficacy of self-care is affected by the ability to assimilate and use information about health status and disease risk (Levin and Idler, 1981). It is, therefore, necessary to investigate not only existing levels of health knowledge, but also the factors which facilitate the assimilation and use of health information. The effectiveness of mutual aid groups in this regard is a particularly important topic to investigate.

Differences in cultural background are known to influence both the experience of and responses to illness (WHO, 1980; Zola, 1966). More extensive data on the influence of cultural variations are needed. Finally, little is known about the effects of health system organisation on the range of self-care behaviour. Cross-national comparisons will contribute valuable information regarding the relevant influence of cultural and health system organisation on self-care practices.

Chronic illness

While individual and family care provide the foundation of health maintenance and acute condition management, it is in the management of chronic illness that the role of self and family care are the most obvious (Levin and Idler, 1981). For some conditions such as diabetes, self-care is the major determinant of outcome. Diabetics must learn to balance their calorific and insulin intake with their levels of physical exertion. Unexpected events, physical illness or emotional stress may require adjustments in calorific or insulin requirements. Acceptance of the condition, adjustment to and control over management regimes and sensitivity to physiological changes are crucial components of care. The vast majority of resources have been allocated to biomedical research on diabetes while the most readily obtainable gains in treatment may be in self-management of the condition. Diabetics themselves may be the best resource for the design of research instruments to collect valuable behavioural data regarding this condition.

In chronic conditions requiring extensive effort and perseverance to achieve maximum rehabilitation, such as stroke, family and other social support may be a major determinant of effective coping. The continuity inherent in family care may provide an environment of security and reassurance stimulating the patient's motivation for sustained effort and adaptation. On the other hand, investigations should consider not only these mechanisms, but also the effects of chronic illness on family solidarity and functioning. Likewise, possible negative effects of family care must be considered (Levin and Idler, 1981; Litman, 1974). Mutual aid groups may be particularly effective forms of support for coping with the multiple care needs associated with many chronic illnesses.

Chronic conditions once assumed to depend predominantly on professional care are being successfully cared for by patients and their families. Indeed, some medical care experts consider recent developments in patient self-care and mutual aid as among the more promising innovations in treatment (Levin et al, 1976). It is now the task of researchers to chart these developments. Evaluative research investigations are needed to determine the extent to which the promise is being realised and to identify factors which may impede progress.

Priorities for research

Since there is so little systematic knowledge about self-care it is appropriate to conclude with an agenda for future research. Self-care behaviour in the context of the primary self-help group, the family, is perhaps the most fruitful topic. The establishment of an information base which can be used in effective programme development requires careful elaboration of the distributions and relative influence of a number of variables:

1. types of family structure associated with alternative patterns of self-care behaviour;
2. types of support provided by various family members during illness;
3. illness conditions associated with alternative patterns of self and family care;
4. effects of community services on family patterns of self-care;
5. effects of family care of chronic illness on family solidarity and functioning.

The function of social networks in the health maintenance and illness response behaviour of individuals is a second priority area for self-care research. While related to family support, social network is a broader concept and should be the central focus of research investigations. Topics of special importance to include in these investigations are the support and network functions of mutual aid groups.

The interface between self-care and mutual aid groups is a third research area. Likewise, the interface between self/family care and professional care is a subject about which virtually nothing is known. Knowledge of the interactions and forces shaping the interactions between the levels of care is a prerequisite for enhancing the functioning of the different levels of care.

The relationship between age and health care behaviour is a subject which needs independent analysis. Identification of the forces shaping female responses to illness also requires separate investigation.

The influence of beliefs and attitudes on self-care behaviour needs clarification. While extensive data on health beliefs and preventive health behaviour have been collected, problems of definition and methodology often make the findings difficult to compare and confusing. Less attention has been directed towards the role of health beliefs in behavioural responses to illness. Two types of investigations concerned with attitudes toward self-care are needed:

1. studies of lay beliefs regarding the factors which produce health;
2. studies of professional beliefs regarding self-care.

References and relevant literature

Aarhus (1979) Loegekredsforengingen for Aarhus amt., Sygdomsmonstret i almen praksis, Aahus Amtskommunes Trykkeri.

Anderson, J., Buck, C., Danaher, K. and Fry, J. (1977) 'Users and Non-users of Doctors: Implications for self-care', Journal of the Royal College of General Practitioners, 27, 155.

Arie, T. (1977) 'Issues in the Psychiatric Care of the Elderly', in A.N. Exton-Smith and J.G. Evans (eds.), Care of the Elderly: Meeting the Challenge of Dependency, Academic Press, London.

Battistella,R. (1971) 'Factors Associated with Delay in the Initiation of Physicians' Care among Late Adulthood Persons', American Journal of Public Health, 61, 1348.

Becker,M. (1974) The Health Belief Model and Personal Health Behaviour, Charles B. Slack Inc., New Jersey.

Belloc, N.B.L. (1972) 'Relationship of Physical Health Status and Health Practices', Preventive Medicine, 1, 409.

Birren, J. and Renner, V. (1980) 'Concepts and Issues of Mental Health and Ageing' in J. Birren and R. Sloane (eds.), Handbook of Mental Health and Ageing, Prentice-Hall Inc., New Jersey.

Breslow, L. and Engstrom, J.E. (1980) 'Persistence of Health Habits and their Relationships to Mortality', Preventive Medicine, 9, 469.

Carlsen, H., Christiansen, F. and Holst, E. (1971) 'Drug Consumption in Denmark', Acta Socio-Medica Scandinavia, 2, 121.

Davis, M. (1966) 'Variations in Patients' Compliance with Doctors' Orders: Analysis of Congruence between Survey Responses and Results of Empirical Investigations', Journal of Medical Education, 41, 1037.

Dean, K. (1980) 'Analysis of the Relationships between Social and Demographic Factors and Self-care Patterns in the Danish Population', unpublished PhD dissertation, University of Minnesota.

Dean, K. (1981) 'Self-care Responses to Illness: a selected overview', Social Science and Medicine, 15a, 673.

Dunnell, K. and Cartwright, A. (1972) Medicine Takers, Prescribers and Hoarders, Routledge Kegan Paul, London.

Fiske, M. (1980) 'Tasks and Crises of the Second Half of Life: The Interrelationship of Commitment, Coping and Adaptation', in J. Birren and R. Sloane (eds.), op.cit..

Gaity, C. and Vamer, R. (1980) 'Preventive Aspects of Mental Illness in Late Life', in J. Birren and R. Sloane (eds.), op.cit..

Gannik,D. and Jespersen, M. (1980) 'Rygbesvoer og sygdomsadfoerd', Nordisk Medicin, 95, 247.

Knapp, D. and Knapp, D. (1972) 'Decision-making and Self-medication', American Journal of Hospital Pharmacy, 29, 1004.

Levin, L., Katz, A. and Holst, E. (1976) Self-care, Prodist, New York.

Levin, L. and Idler, E. (1981) The Hidden Health Care System, Ballinger Publishing Co., Cambridge.

Litman, T. (1971) 'Health Care and the Family: a three generation analysis', Medical Care, 9, 67.

Litman, T. (1974) 'Health Care and the Family: a behavioural overview', Social Science and Medicine, 8, 495.

Marston, M. (1970) 'Compliance with Medical Regimes: a review of the literature', Nursing Research, 19, 312.

McKeown, T. (1976) The Role of Medicine: Dream, Mirage or Nemesis?, Nuffield Provincial Hospitals Trust, London.

McKinlay, J. (1972) 'Some Approaches and Problems in the Study of the Use of Services: An overview', Journal of Health and Social Behaviour, 13, 115.

McKinlay, J. and McKinlay, S. (1978) 'The Questionable Contribution of Medical Measures to the Decline of Mortality in the United States in the Twentieth Century', Health and Society, The Milbank Memorial Fund Quarterly, 55, 405.

Pedersen, P. (1976) 'Patienters selvebehandling inden henvendelse til praktiserende loege', Ugeskrift for loeger, 138, 1955.

Rabin, D. and Bush, P. (1975) 'Who's Using Medications?', Journal of Comparative Health, 1, 106.

Risse, G., Numbers, R. and Leariff, J. (eds.) (1977) Present State and Future Needs of General Practice, 3rd ed., Reports from General Practice, No.16, Royal College of General Practitioners, London.

Snider, E. (1980) 'Awareness and Use of Health Services by the Elderly', Medical Care, 18, 1177.

Stimson, G. (1974) 'Obeying Doctors' Orders: a view from the other side', Social Science and Medicine, 8, 97.

Williamson, J. and Danaher, K. (1978) Self-care in Health, Croom Helm, London.

World Health Organization (1980) The Wellbeing of the World's Ageing Citizens: a status report, WHO, Geneva.

Zola, I. (1966) 'Culture and Symptoms: an analysis of patients presenting complaints', American Sociological Review, 31, 615.

THE DIVERSITY OF SELF-HELP GROUPS
Ann Richardson

Introduction

The past decade has witnessed a great proliferation of mutual aid (or 'self-help') groups in many countries, concerned with a wide variety of medical, behavioural and social conditions. Despite the evident heterogeneity of the problems on which they are focussed, these groups are generally thought to conform to a roughly similar pattern. There seems to be a clear image of what constitutes a mutual aid group in the public mind. They are composed of people with a single common problem who have joined together to provide a common solution to it. Everyone is fully involved and committed. They work by members giving help to one another on a mutual, reciprocal basis. They share, in short, a common framework, whatever the problem to which they are devoted.

The aim of this paper is to demonstrate that this picture of mutual aid groups is much too simple. It may prove correct in some cases, of course, but the reality of what self-help groups do, why members join and what they gain from their involvement, is much more complex. Members do not necessarily share a common diagnosis of their problem nor a common view of how to cope with it. Their involvement and sense of commitment to their group is not always very great. And, whatever their belief in the value of reciprocity, members' ability to put it into practice is severely constrained. It is necessary to move beyond the rhetoric and take a deeper look at self-help groups in practice.

The ideas and data presented here are derived from research on four mutual aid organisations in England. These were all composed of people with primarily social, rather than medical or psychological, problems: lone parents, widows, women caring for elderly or infirm dependants (known as 'carers') and parents of mentally handicapped children and adults. All were national organisations with a network of local groups. The study collected information both on local group activities and problems and on members' involvement and assessment of them. This paper draws especially on the latter aspect of the study, which included both a postal survey of a random sample of members and some supplementary interviews. Fuller information on this study can be found elsewhere (Richardson and Goodman, 1983). Although these results are derived from groups whose focus was other than medical problems, there is no obvious reason to believe that they

32

are not equally applicable to specifically health-oriented self-help groups. It is the <u>analysis</u>, rather than the specific data, which enables general conclusions to be drawn.

The activities of self-help groups

Before members' reasons for joining and degree of involvement can be discussed, it is necessary to consider briefly what mutual aid groups actually do. Although they are best known for holding meetings in which members can discuss common problems and gain emotional support, these groups generally do much more than this. Indeed, there are five separate kinds of help which groups provide members.

1. Emotional support. People with problems tend to feel lonely, confused and isolated, and it helps to talk about these problems with others 'in the same boat'. Such support may be provided communally or on an individual basis. It may be aimed at helping the individual to adjust to his situation or to change it. It may be offered primarily in a crisis or it may be available over a longer term.

2. Information and advice. For most conditions around which self-help groups are formed, there is information which will help people cope more easily. Such information and advice may concern methods of self-care or cure, or it may concern benefits or services provided by statutory or other organisations. Groups may give advice themselves or direct members to other sources, or both.

3. Direct services. Some forms of help needed to cope with particular problems can be provided directly by mutual aid organisations. These may be provided on a casual or informal basis, such as babysitting or running errands for the housebound, or they may be provided more formally, such as established playgroups or holiday play schemes. They may be carried out by group members on a voluntary basis or they may involve hired staff; a few groups even provide services jointly with their local authority.

4. Social activities. While the provision of an active social life could be seen as a pleasant sideline to the main purpose of self-help groups, many groups themselves consider this an integral part of what they do for members, particularly where the condition itself entails considerable loneliness. Some social activities may be specially arranged occasions, such as coach outings, but an active social life may also be provided simply through regular group meetings.

5. Pressure group activities. Many self-help groups consider the benefits or services provided by statutory authorities to their members to be inadequate, and therefore take some measures to bring about change. Some groups aim to develop a collaborative relationship with authorities in the pursuit of

their cause, while others prefer an adversary role. Some organisations are primarily concerned to publicise the nature of the problems suffered by their members, attempting to influence general opinion rather than a specific statutory audience.

Contrary to the impression given by some early writings on this subject,(e.g.Tracey and Gussow, 1976 and Gartner and Riessman, 1977) these activities are not typically seen as alternatives by mutual aid groups themselves. Most try to provide all of them at one time or another, although not necessarily simultaneously or organised by the same people. Furthermore, the nature of the help provided often varies within individual groups; different kinds of support, different kinds of social activity, and different targets of political work may all be encompassed by a single group. One must be cautious in ascribing to groups a single purpose or function.

If a common problem leads to a single obvious solution, how does this heterogeneity of activity come about? One answer is that many problems have in fact more than one solution and groups naturally try to meet members' needs in as many ways as they can. Thus, some make available support and social activities to members while also trying to increase services provided for them by statutory agencies. More fundamentally, however, many conditions entail a series of different problems, so that people with a 'common' condition may not in fact address themselves to the same basic problem at all. In other words, people ostensibly 'in the same boat' may actually need or want very different kinds of help. These divergent aims can arise because of varying attitudes to the problem or because members are at different stages of a common cycle.

Two examples, taken from groups studied in this research, may serve to illustrate these points. First, lone parents clearly share a common situation in having to care for one or more children without the help of a partner. But they by no means invariably share a single solution to this common 'problem'; some aim solely to come to terms with their situation, some aim to alleviate it by gaining more benefits and services and some aim to rid themselves of it entirely by finding a new partner. Furthermore, some lone parents are primarily concerned to gain help for their children, whereas others have a greater need of help for themselves. In sum, although they find themselves with a common label, lone parents do not invariably have common problems or common aspirations at all. This heterogeneity of aims and intentions leads to a heterogeneity of activities within individual groups.

Secondly, the problems faced by people with a common condition often change over time. To give one example, parents of new-born mentally handicapped children all tend to face similar emotional and practical difficulties, but their needs and those of their children change as the children grow older. The aims and needs of elderly parents of middle-aged handicapped 'children' bear little resemblance to those of young parents of handicapped babies. The aims and needs of parents of school-aged children or young adults are different still. Again, although they share a common label, parents of mentally handicapped children do not inevitably have common problems at all. Again, this means that self-help groups for such parents tend to try to provide a range of different activities and forms of help for their members.

Why members join

Why, then, do members join self-help groups? Given the many different sorts of help which they provide, what serves as the principal attraction? Table 1 illustrates the wide range of help sought by members of the four organisations studied. It can be seen that some sought the general companionship of others in their situation and emotional support, some sought social activities for themselves or their children and some sought information and other forms of practical help. In addition, some joined in order to work to help others with their particular problem. Many joined with a number of different aims.

Table 1: <u>Reasons for joining group</u>

Percentages giving following answers	Parents of MHC	Lone Parents	Widows	Carers
	per cent	per cent	per cent	per cent
To meet others in the same situation	47	78	72	30
Understanding and support	36	33	25	33
Social activities for self	-	51	56	14
Social activities for child/ children	34	56	-	-
Information/advice	51	27	22	41
Practical help of services	31	14	8	20
To work to improve situation of people with the problem	45	16	44	44
Nothing in particular	8	4	5	11
Base	607	430	553	619

Note: The question read 'When you <u>first</u> joined your (self-help group), what were the <u>main</u> things you were looking for?' Answers were pre-coded, but others could be added. There was no limit to the number of answers members could give.

It is, in fact, difficult to summarise these data because there are few common patterns. Members of the two organisations whose principal focus was loss of a marriage partner (lone parents and widows) gave much greater stress to companionship and social activities. In the words of members interviewed, 'You need people around you to realise it's not happened just to you', 'You feel a social outcast; you need to know there's somebody else who cares'. Members of the other two organisations were more concerned to gain various forms of practical help and advice. Again, in the words of members interviewed, 'Information - how other people had got on with the same problems'; 'They know all the snags that have cropped up'. Interestingly, very similar proportions of three of the four groups indicated their concern to work to help others.

But these data are themselves very rough, referring to all members of each organisation in turn. When disaggregated by the nature of the situation faced by members at the time they joined, even greater variations can be noted. It is often assumed that people join self-help groups only at the moment of crisis - when their husband dies, handicapped child is born and so forth. This is far from the case. Over half the members of all but one of the organisations had been living with the particular problem for over two years at the time they joined, and for many the relevant period was much longer - ten or even twenty years. (The exception was the group for single parents, half of whose members had joined within one year of finding themselves on their own.) Whatever the reasons for the long delay, its effect was to bring together people at very different stages of their ostensibly common situation.

Take the fairly straightforward example of widows. About one-third had joined their group within a year of bereavement, one-third had joined between one and five years afterwards, and one-third had joined when they had been widowed for at least five years. Not surprisingly, the desire for companionship with other widows, though strong among all members, declined as a reason for joining as the duration of widowhood increased. In other words, this was a strong motivation among the newly bereaved (expressed by 83 per cent) but less strong among those who had been widowed for some time (expressed by 64 per cent). In members' own words, a newly widowed woman stressed, 'Other widows are the only ones who can understand'; whereas a widow of some duration saw the group in a much less unique light: 'I join everything; the widows' group is only once a month'. In contrast, those who joined some time after their bereavement were somewhat more concerned to work to improve the situation of widows generally than were the newly bereaved. They were, presumably, in less need of direct help themselves and more able to think about working to help others.

Levels of involvement

People join self-help groups then, for a great variety of reasons, varying both with the nature of their general condition and with their particular circumstances within it. But what does this mean for their subsequent involvement in their group? Once firmly ensconced as members, do they all then follow a roughly similar experience? Again, contrary to common assumptions, the answer is clearly negative. The nature of members' involvement - what they give to and get from their group - varies enormously both between groups and between members within them. This can be illustrated in terms of both members' sense of involvement and the amount of help they claim to have given and received from their group.

Table 2 shows the level of involvement members of all four organisations indicated with respect to their group. Most claimed to be neither highly active nor wholly inactive but put themselves somewhere in between. Again, members of the two organisations who were most concerned to gain companionship and an active social life (lone parents and widows) indicated a higher general level of involvement. More members of the other two organisations claimed to be inactive, while being happy to know the group was there. Members of the organisation for carers of dependent relatives were noticeably inactive.

Again, however, these data do not demonstrate the extent of variation within groups. Just as not all members join at the same point with respect to their problem, so too, not all current members have experienced the condition for the same length of time. Activity levels tended to vary, sometimes considerably, with the duration both of membership and of the problem itself. In the case of parents of mentally handicapped children, for instance, long-term members tended to be much more active than recent recruits; a sizeable proportion (17 per cent) of the former claimed to be highly active, whereas only very few (two per cent) of the latter claimed to be so. (These data refer to members of ten or more years' duration and members of less than two years' duration respectively.) This was partly, but not wholly, a function of the age of their child, those with young children being less able to play an active role. It can also be taken as an indication of their greater commitment to the group, generated over time.

Table 2:   Members' sense of involvement in their group

Percentages giving following answers	Parents of MHC	Lone Parents	Widows	Carers
	per cent	per cent	per cent	per cent
Highly committed and active	14	11	9	5
Active/attend regularly	16	33	38	15
Somewhat active/attend occasionally	26	25	13	15
Inactive but like knowing group 'is there'	34	19	26	46
Inactive/little interest	2	2	3	8
No longer involved	4	10	9	8
Base	607	430	553	619

Note: The question read 'Which of the following best describes your current level of involvement with your (self-help group)?'. The answers were pre-coded and somewhat more detailed than shown here.

Members also varied in the extent to which they felt they had given help to or received help from other members of their group. Table 3 shows the responses of members of the four organisations to questions on this matter. The majority of members of two groups (parents of mentally handicapped children and lone parents) felt they had both given and received help through their groups, whereas only a minority of members of the other two groups felt this to be the case. These variations reflect, in part, differential needs of the members of the respective groups; both parents of handicapped children and lone parents might be seen to be more likely to need practical help and information than the others, although this is by no means obviously the case. It should be added that many more members of all groups may have given and received help at meetings, without labelling it as such. 'Mutual aid' is often a matter of very inexplicit give and take; as one widow said, quite simply, 'Friends help friends'.

Although there was some variation in response to both of these questions within each organisation, one particular pattern is especially noteworthy. The propensity to give help was regularly greater among those who had experienced the relevant problem for some time compared with those who were new to it. (The one exception here was the parents of mentally handicapped children, where roughly similar proportions of all parents said that they helped others.) Thus, in the case of lone parents, considerably more of those who had been on their own for at least five years (74 per cent) said they had given help than those who had been in this situation for less than two years (57 per cent). This finding is not at all surprising; people who are trying to cope with a wholly new and difficult situation are much less able to give help to others than those with considerable experience of it. Furthermore, the latter are much more likely to have a sense of commitment to help others in their situation. As one newly active woman said of her group, 'It has given me a sense of identity; I want to do the same for other people who are just joining ... I would like to do more in order to pay back what I have received'.

Table 3:   Help received and given by members

Percentages giving following answers	Parents of MHC	Lone Parents	Widows	Carers
	per cent	per cent	per cent	per cent
Received help from group:				
Information on benefits/services		52	33	30
Advice on personal problem	10	22	4	10
Practical help	30	25	3	8
None/no answer	37	45	65	59
Given help to members of group:				
Information on benefits/services		27	18	14
Advice on personal problem	23	46	21	14
Practical help	41	47	20	18
None/no answer	44	30	61	70
Base	607	430	553	619

Note: The questions read 'Have you ever received any of the following forms of help from your (self-help group)?' and 'Have you ever given help to other members of your (self-help group)? What forms of help have you given?'. The answers were pre-coded and somewhat more detailed than shown here. If help had been received or given, one to three forms could be indicated; the fourth answer shows all those who gave no positive indication of receiving or giving help.

Securing serial reciprocity

A belief in the importance of reciprocity clearly underlies the very existence of self-help groups. It is, indeed, the principal quality which is often said to distinguish them from more conventional sources of support. Yet it can be seen that despite members' desire to give mutual aid, their ability to do so is severely constrained. Members do not come together on an equal basis; they have not only unequal needs with respect to their problem but unequal resources for handling it as well. The crucial factor here is time; the longer a person has had a problem, the longer he will have had to learn to cope with it. He will have learned his way around external sources of help and gained insight into the best ways of dealing with the problem himself. Whether through membership of the self-help group itself or via other means, those who have had a condition for some time are likely to have gained valuable experience with respect to it.

This experience is an important resource for all self-help groups. If it is not always possible to effect full mutuality of assistance, as posited here, it is clearly desirable to muster the help of those with experience of the problem, whatever their current needs. It might, indeed, be argued that self-help groups work best through this 'serial reciprocity', whereby individuals join in order to get help, receive it, and then remain to pass on help to others. While the assistance is not directly reciprocal (between members at the same time), it is serially so. The emphasis on reciprocity can be maintained, despite the day-to-day presence of some 'giving' and some 'receiving' members.

In order to effect such reciprocity, however, groups need both to retain their experienced members and to ensure a sense of commitment among them. Unfortunately, groups vary considerably in their ability to do this. Some organisations retain the loyalty of members not only long after they need any direct help but even long after they have the 'problem' at all. The great majority of members of the organisation for women caring for dependent relatives, for instance, were former - rather than current - carers, who had remained members after their dependant had died. Other organisations, in contrast, suffer a high turnover, with members leaving once the initial period of crisis has passed. Only one-third of the members of the organisation for lone parents, for instance, had belonged to their group for over two years. Whether the others left happily, having been helped, or not, is not clear, but one effect of their departure was to diminish a vitally important component of the resources available to the organisation.

What can self-help groups do to encourage such members to remain? There is, regrettably, no magic formula here. The propensity of members to leave is often a function not of the activities of individual groups, but of the condition for which they were formed. Lone parents, for instance, are not only younger and more mobile than women caring for elderly dependants, but also more likely to change their status dramatically through remarriage. The commitment members feel for others in their situation is similarly not the same for all conditions and for all organisations. It varies with the severity and duration of the problem as well as with the degree of mutual identification which groups can generate among their members. Organisations formed around certain demanding and long-standing conditions will find such commitment readily available. Others will have to place particular emphasis on creating it by careful attention to members' needs and positive encouragement of active member involvement. Where such commitment can be generated or harnessed, it can prove one of the most valuable assets of a self-help group.

Conclusions

Self-help groups vary in many different ways and it is not possible in a short paper to do justice to all of them. A few key sources of diversity have been explored here. It has been shown that members join for different reasons, have different patterns of involvement and retain their membership for different lengths of time. The effect of these decisions is to create wide variations in the activities and atmosphere of self-help groups, and in the long run to affect the very longevity of groups themselves.

These conclusions, while derived from research on four organisations concerned with social care, have much wider applicability. It can be surmised that self-help groups focussed on health problems will also vary strikingly between one another in what they do, why members join and the extent and level of members' involvement. They, too, will display varying abilities to generate serial reciprocity among their membership and thus ensure they are a source of continuing help. Such variations are unlikely to be wholly random, but arise from certain characteristics of their members and the nature of the condition for which they were formed. We have drawn attention to a few key variables here.

This diversity is not simply a matter for academic interest; it affects real people joining, organising and trying to assist self-help groups in practice. It is essential for all those concerned with such groups, whether as members or as sympathetic outsiders, to appreciate the complexity of mutual aid - both its benefits and its limitations. They must expect to find not one form of help but many different ones; not one common experience or pattern of growth but many different ones. 'Self-help' has become a single label, but it masks a wide variety of diverse developments.

References

Gartner, Alan and Riessman, Frank (1977) Self-help in the Human Services, Jossey-Bass, San Franciso.

Richardson, Ann and Goodman, Meg (1983) <u>Self-help and Social Care: Mutual aid Organisations in Practice</u>, Policy Studies Institute, London.

Tracey, George S. and Gussow, Zachary (1976) 'Self-help Groups: a grass roots response to a need for services', <u>Journal of Applied Behavioural Sciences</u>, 12.

GROUPES DE SANTÉ: THE USERS' MOVEMENT IN FRANCE
Alf Trojan

Why should a foreigner write about self-help in France? The answer is simple. The concept of self-help does not exist in France, nor is there a term, other than perhaps the rather long-winded expression prise en charge par soi-même, to define it.(1) Due to this lack of a theoretical concept, French people can hardly recognise the empirical phenomenon. Consequently, they usually reply in the negative to all questions concerning the existence of self-help groups in France, usually by adding their favourite explanation: 'French people are too individualistic for things like that'. There are also four other, and in my opinion, less important reasons for the alleged non-existence of shgs: the groups are often part of another context than health care or of another social movement; they are a relatively new phenomenon; there seem to be fewer self-help discussion groups in France than in many other European countries; their social visibility is less, because neither the media nor research is interested in this phenomenon.

My first general confirmation that self-help associations actually existed in France was a kind of directory: Alternatives, No.6/7: Ressources Speciales (1978). This is a compilation of various announcements, book reviews and short articles. The section on health mentions journals of the consumer movement in France, organisations of left doctors and fringe medicine, topics like natural childbirth, cancer, dying and so on. Within this context I found my first examples of self-help associations: Groupe de Malades Auto-organisé; Boutique de Santé; Ligue Nationale pour la Liberté des Vaccinations; La Fondation Internationale d'Assistance de Défense et d'Information des Malades; Handicapes méchants; and so on. During the following weeks I tried to discover and to understand the French health movement.(2) The results of about two months of investigation will be presented in this article. My research experience in Hamburg shows, however, that after two months one still tends to underestimate the real number of groups, and that it is impossible to get a clear picture of all features of the self-help spectrum.

I start with a description of the major groups and events related to the development of self-help in France. A second part contains some generalising remarks and looks for explanations of this development. In the third, final part, I attempt a comparison of the situation in France and West Germany.

I The Development of the Users' Movement

I shall not go too far back to all the roots of this movement. Most of the activities mentioned below started during the mid-1970s. From the first period after May 1968, that is, from the early 1970s, one should mention the GIS (Groupe Information Santé). This group was composed of medics and non-medics, originating from the more informal rather than organised part of the 1968 movement and working on a less theoretical basis, particularly at local level and in the field of occupational medicine. This group has influenced many of the people who now work in other groups more fully described below. An article in Autrement (1977, p.86) calls this group 'la mère nourricière des mouvements de contestation'.

The consumer movement and the journal L'Impatient

In 1974 two books appeared about pharmaceutical drugs and the pharmaceutical industry. L'Invasion Pharmaceutique by Dupuy and Karsenty and the Guide des médicaments les plus courants by Pradal are critical accounts of the quantitatively most relevant aspect of medical practice, the prescription of drugs. Owing to a criminal case started by the pharmaceutical industry against Dr. Pradal, as well as through public debates jointly organised by Karsenty and Pradal, the media gave great attention to these books. Consumer awareness of the need for more critical use of drugs has been growing steadily since then. At about the same time the effects of the two books were reinforced (and the consumer approach extended to other medical services) by the two biggest consumer journals 50 millions and Que Choisir? (see Busseau, 1980).

In November 1977 Dr. Pradal and others launched L'Impatient, a journal for the defence and information of the consumer of medical services. Locating itself explicitly in the tradition of consumerism, the editorial of issue number one mentions as its first goal, 'to make known the existing associations of defense and the initiatives they take'. The other goals are to provide information on consumers' rights, scandals of malpractice, effective therapies including all types of fringe medicine (médecine douces, naturelles, paralleles) and practical advice on self-help. These functions of the journal represent support for those 'courageous doctors' who are opposed to the medical establishment but are 'too few to really change things'.

To date more than fifty issues of L'Impatient have appeared; the journal has about 20,000 subscribers. The first issue contained reports on groups for the defense of hospital patients, number four on patients' organisations ('Des Malades Autonomes'). Subsequent numbers have repeatedly offered to help existing groups and support the formation of new groups.(3)

General practioners of the 'SMG'

The Syndicat de la Médecine Généraliste (an organisation of about 500 general practitioners) was founded in 1975. Like other groups that emphasise the health user's importance, the SMG dates back to the 1968 movement (see Autrement 1977). Their main goal is the establishment of 'unites sanitaires de base' (local health centres). This concept corresponds closely to the WHO strategy for primary health care. The French concept evisaged for the community ('les usagers') is not only participation but also 'control' of their local services.

In 1979 a special issue of the monthly journal of the SMG tried to evaluate the experience of group practices and health centres that had 'users' associations. Nearly all of these groups were initiated by professionals after an annual meeting of the SMG in 1977. Their main purposes are health education and prevention through public meetings and debates on selected topics like contraception, diet, menopause, mental diseases and doctor-patient relationships. Only rarely did independent self-help groups emerge, working continuously on a specific problem.(4)

In spite of the many problems (widespread passivity, lack of financial support, lack of political influence), Annie-Claire Deyon (1979) concludes her compilation with the sentence, 'We are not poor lonesome toubibs (doctors) any more!' - a view shared in a preface in L'Impatient, (that is, their counterparts) about the SMG which states: 'They merit support from us'. The relationship between users and the SMG is conceived of as one of mutual help and mutual education.

Boutiques de santé (health shops)

In order to help people who had been accused of political involvement in the 1968 movement, Boutiques de Droit came into existence. Modelled on these, the first Boutique de Santé was opened in January 1977 in Tours. The mains goals were to change the helper-client relationship and to enable users to take over the responsibility for themselves. The members mainly provided a certain amount of consulting time. The question was, what user demands could emerge when professionals themselves do not stimulate such demands? In accordance with the hypothesis included in this question, no clearcut demands were manifested by the users. The experiment came to an end after about one year - but others continued. In several arrondissements of Paris, Boutiques de Santé were opened; the first ones being in the 10th, and shortly after, in the 13th and 9th arrondissements. Most of these and similar experiments do not exist any more. They have either become part of paid community social work or else they are in a phase of redefining their goals. They were mainly action groups of politically motivated professionals who organised public debates and provided information on health problems. Attempts to involve the local residents in their activities were usually rather disappointing.

The Groupe Santé du 9e is in many ways an exception. This group is based mainly on non-professional members; the weekly debates organised by them are well attended and have sometimes led to the creation of independent groups (for example, cancer, asthma patients). It is difficult to explain completely the outstanding success of this group, but obviously it is to a large degree due to its co-founder and 'animatrice', Liliane Leflaive, a former Red Cross nurse, who has dedicated a great deal of her time and capacities to this group.(5)

'Autrement' and the alternative movement

Anybody looking for alternative approaches in the various social areas should start reading some of the guides published by Editions Alternatives et Paralleles and the daily advertisements and announcements in Libération, a journal founded in the early 1970s as a corollary to the 1968 movement. Though the alternative movement in France is often regarded as nearly non-existent (being seen as too new, too small, or different in its nature) it has, nevertheless, an excellent source of support, the project 'Autrement'. Created in 1975 as a tool for observing and inspiring social change, it publishes a monthly journal, dossiers on specific topics, alternative guides for the bigger cities and some French 'départements', and organises debates, workshops and conferences, 'in order to analyse new socio-cultural trends and new social practices and to locate and make contact between groups and individuals in alternative experiences' (see Self-help Spotlight, 1979).

After an Autrement publication on new professional approaches in health care (1977), a special issue was produced in September 1980 on their counterparts, the users, and their attempts to gain more autonomy. This issue was followed by public discussions and a two-day conference in Rennes on 'Users and Health' (November 1980). The subsequent report recognised that the 150-odd participants, in spite of their heterogeneity, were part of the same movement.

What struck me as an interesting observation was the distinction made between users ('usagers') and the ill ('les malades') and of the gap between them. The report's conclusion refers to the difficulties health shops and group practices have in involving users and mentions in contrast that autonomous associations (diabetics being an example) originate nearly spontaneously.

The national federation of groups of health users

The meeting in Rennes was followed by two others, the first being organised by the Group Santé du 9e in June 1981. The 'health groups' (by now the most often used general term) met in Paris;

they decided to create a federation and to formulate a charter. The second meeting was in October 1981 in Chambery. The national federation was founded by representatives of about 25 existing groups (mostly users associations and health shops) and others who were just starting a group. The aims of the federation (FeNGUS) are:

1. to be a liaising body for the groups; to initiate and support new groups;
2. to promote their means of action and information;
3. to represent them nationally and internationally;
4. to become an acknowledged and representative force of health care users, without, however, interfering with the local autonomy and originality retained by each group or with its power to make decisions and to run independently.

The first talks with the different ministries in order to get public funding for the employment of a secretary were promising. The result of the distribution of over 2,000 copies of the 'charter' was overwhelming: several hundred requests for a copy of the 'charter', about 300 people wanting to join a group, about 100 wanting to found groups in their own regions and lots of other requests and proposals.(6)

The voluntary sector (la vie associative)
According to a recent bibliography (772 references), there are at present between three and five hundred thousand associations in France (Bruneau and Rioux, 1980), comprising what is called 'la vie associative' or 'le mouvement associatif'. To a large degree the voluntary sector is part of this movement. A recent article by Couste (1981) states that in France volunteering has received a fresh impetus since 1968 and that the role of the 'user' has changed to that of 'participant'.

In 1975 the umbrella organisation DAP (Association pour le Développement des Associations de Progrès) was founded in order to mobilise support for the voluntary sector. The criteria of what constitutes 'associations of progress' are in their most important aspects rather similar to those of self-help organisations: improvement of shared life conditions, no profit, being run according to democratic rules, and so on.

In 1981 the DAP was transformed into a new organisation: 'FONDAtion pour la vie associative'. Among its goals, one finds, above all, the promotion of associations through support services. FONDA's present activities relate in large measure to the discussion and improvement of the government's draft for the reform of the Loi 1901, the law which regulates and recognises registered associations or charities of public benefit.(7)

Among the member associations of FONDA one finds associations of parents of the handicapped and other organisations of and for people with chronic diseases. This part of the self-help spectrum seems to have developed outside the users' movement. On the other hand, I got the impression that the meeting in Rennes had raised the awareness of groups of people 'who suffer from the same diseases and unite in order to help each other mutually, to seek information about treatments, ... to break up the isolation, not to be lonely, but to meet other people to talk and to support each other' (see Clermont, 1981).

II Reasons for the Development of Self-help Groups in France

It soon became obvious to me that there exist many interrelationships between the consumer movement, the journal L'Impatient, professionals of the group practices and health centres belonging to SMG, health shops and the creation of the federation of users' groups (the alternative project Autrement functioning as a catalyst). Somewhat apart from this field of action, one can observe the development of the 'vie associative', which is in effect the voluntary sector, and which includes among many others the associations of and for the handicapped and the chronically ill.

Looking at the field of health care

Analytically, it is possible to distinguish three main purposes in the development of the users' movement.

1. To provide a critique of and impetus to change medical (and political) structures. This is more or less explicitly announced in the users' associations of group practices and in the (former) health shops. The radical professionals who started these groups were looking for political allies against the conservative mainstream of their profession. Improving the patient's self-reliance (prise en mains, prise en charge) meant basically changing the patient in order to change medical (and political) structures.

2. To control and improve medical products and services. This is most clearly to be found in the consumer movement and the journal L'Impatient.

3. To complement existing medical products and services. This view is presented by L'Impatient and the alternative movement, in so far as they inform about and promote natural cures, fringe medicine, various new methods of psychotherapy and personal growth. This complementary function is also a prominent element - though not the only one - of associations of and for the handicapped and the chronically ill.

The change-inducing function and the control function go together without any difficulties, but both remain somewhat separate from the complementary function. The people active in these fields acknowledge each other respectfully or even sympathetically, but often the more political ones, representing the change and control function, look down upon those supporting the complementary function. An amalgamation of the three functions was observable within the Groupe Santé du 9e and the journal L'Impatient. Reports about the first meetings of the federation of users' groups as well as their charter indicate that the federation wants to further integrate the three functions and steps have already been taken to do so. As the Groupe Santé du 9e and L'Impatient are among the most flourishing innovative groups, one can assume that a multifunctional, pluralistic approach is the best means for the Federation to become a useful body for the groups and an influential representative of their interests.

A look at the development of the users' movement shows two periods of heightened activity. The first period started in 1975 with the foundation of organisations which later had an important catalytic function for the creation of health groups (SMG, Autrement) and ended in 1977/78 with the start of the journal L'Impatient and the creation of nearly all of the users associations and health shops. The second period of increased activity started in 1980 with the publication of Autrement's dossier on patients and users of health care. Similarly, Liliane Leflaive characterised the first generation of groups as being mostly created and organised by professionals. The groups of the second generation have a stronger tendency to autonomy, are created by the users themselves, still have professional members, but collaborate with them on a more equal basis (see Clermont, 1981). This very much confirms my own impression, though it is probably true that many of the groups in the Federation might not have started without the stimulation or catalytic support from the helping professions.

The two development phases can be placed within the context of national political developments. By 1975 the 'période gauchistè was over (that is, the period of many - mostly dogmatic - political groups, which originated from the 1968 movement). This vacuum favoured the creation of new organisations. An additional factor is seen in the euphoria preceding the elections of Mach 1978, because many expected a victory of the left. A great number of groups were started during this phase, but after the defeat of the left many active members withdrew, leaving only a small core to continue (see Perthuis, 1980). The most important activities during the second phase took place before and after the election of May 1981, which ended with the 'changement', a new government of left parties.

Looking at the voluntary sector

Publications on the development of the voluntary sector (la vie associative) emphasise two facts (see Bruneau and Rioux, 1981; Couste, 1981):
1. a considerable growth in the number of associations and the social areas covered by them;

2.   a renewal of its nature which can be characterised by a general claim of increased participation and autonomy.

These trends can be observed in most European countries. The French health movement is also due to and part of this general development. The roots of this development are to be sought in more secular trends of modern industrial societies: more and more alienated work, bureaucratised political and inhuman social institutions, expropriation of personal coping capacities through the growing predominance of professional experts.

My impression was that in-so-far as self-help had a more 'political' nature in France, it was more highly esteemed. However, the idea of what constitutes a 'political' nature seems to be limited to direct influence on political parties and institutions. There seems to be a reluctance to recognise the political nature of groups and activities which are committed to personal or allegedly very specific problems. This may be one of the reasons for the existing gap between many users' associations and the groups of the chronically ill (see Autrement, Nov. 1980, p.19), which have their roots more in the voluntary sector.(8)

What about the chances of bridging that gap? According to the three above-mentioned main purposes of the health groups in France, one can also distinguish three traditions from which they stem: the 1968 tradition, the consumer tradition and the volunteer tradition. Recent changes in these traditions have led to the hypothesis of a mutual convergence and amalgamation.

1.   The 1968 tradition led to a first generation of users' associations and health shops. By and large this experience was, for most professionals, more disappointing than encouraging. The second generation of health groups seems to be less political (in the narrow sense, that is, less ambitious to make a direct impact on existing structures and institutions), more interested in alternative therapy approaches based largely on volunteer work by non-professionals.

2.   The consumer tradition is older than the 1968 movement. It started during the 1950s and 1960s as a corollary of economic growth and the immense increase of all sorts of products. Although the consumer movement was very much stimulated by the 1968 movement, it is basically a response to more general features of industrial societies. For this reason, as well as because of its openness to new therapeutic approaches and its concurrence with many of the goals of patient organisations in the voluntary sector, the consumer tradition seems to be present in almost all types of health groups. This may potentially be used as a mediating function for the different traditions.

3.   The volunteer tradition is changing in nature. There is a greater awareness of the hierarchy between those who help and those who are helped. There is more volunteering for

one's own problems (which is identical with self-help). Volunteer commitment less and less means 'charity' and more and more improvement of one's own community, and one's living conditions in a general sense. Thus, the volunteer tradition seems to be getting more political, especially on the local level.

In my opinion, these developments will further diminish the differences between the three traditions and facilitate a growth of the French health movement, which is already based on various types of self-help initiatives and is at the same time the most important catalytic agent for the formation of new groups.

III France and West Germany Compared

Owing to the lack of an internationally accepted classification, I proceed from our(9) last attempt to categorise the spectrum of 'self-help associations' along two dimensions:
1.   closeness to/remoteness from the public/professional system;
2.   self-change versus social change as the main goal;
This leads us to the following diagram (figure 1):

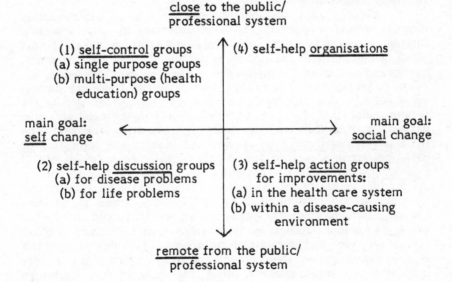

close to the public/ professional system

(1) self-control groups
(a) single purpose groups
(b) multi-purpose (health education) groups

(4) self-help organisations

main goal: self change ← → main goal: social change

(2) self-help discussion groups
(a) for disease problems
(b) for life problems

(3) self-help action groups for improvements:
(a) in the health care system
(b) within a disease-causing environment

remote from the public/ professional system

The classification is an analytical one to help locate self-help associations in a socio-political framework. The empirical reality however is far more complex: none of the self-help associations correspond exactly to the theoretical types; each one has its own position in the four quadrants, and this normally changes during a group's career, often moving from one field to another.

Self-control groups

The goals of these groups are determined by professionals. In order to reduce, for example, risk factors such as smoking, obesity or hypertension, such groups often use behavioural self-control programmes. They concentrate very much on self-change and are closely attached to the professional (for example a practice) or public system, for example, many clubs of former mental patients in Germany.

I know of only a few groups in Germany where this approach really works well. The crucial point seems to be that the motivation to continue such a group is usually missing if a person is not suffering and somebody else is pushing him to do something about his health. In France too I found few examples of this type of group, as far as single purpose groups were concerned (cf. Pratiques nouvelles, 1981; L'Impatient No.16, 1979, p.23). However, many health groups of the first generation (that is, those attached to group practices) seem to be equally influenced by professionals, but because of the non-specifity of their goals (health education in general) they appear to be more similar in their proceedings to the type of group discussed next.

Self-help discussion groups

In these groups the participants help each other mainly through mutual support in terms of information, understanding, sharing of emotional crises, etc. This type of group, which is most often connected with the notion of self-help in the narrow sense, has spread in Germany considerably during the past few years, but seems to be less known in France. Nevertheless, there are enough examples to prove that this type exists in France too: groups for former alcoholics, for obesity (including Weight Watchers), for patients with cancer, asthma, depression and other diseases. The little adverts in L'Impatient sometimes lead to the formation of patients' groups, mostly for people with chronic diseases.(10) Libération publishes most adverts from people wanting to form a group for problems of everyday living (particularly problems centring around loneliness). As in Germany, these groups are normally not known to the public, and I am quite convinced that there are far more groups, many of which must be 'hidden' in other movements such as the feminist movement, which has adopted the English expression 'self-help groups' for groups which practice self-diagnosis and self-treatment along the lines of the American feminist health centres; the gay movement; the movement of the handicapped (which produces a journal of its own); ex-mental patients (whom I got to know through several radio broadcasts); and in the voluntary sector generally.

Self-help action groups

Groups pressing for <u>improvements of the health care system</u> seem to be slightly more frequent in France than in Germany. Most of these groups are part of the consumer movement, which is stronger in France in so far as health services are concerned. In France as well as in Germany some groups have closer connections with the human rights movement, in particular, associations of the handicapped and former mental patients.

A quantitative and qualitative comparison of <u>preventive self-help action groups</u> would require an investigation of its own. It is quite obvious, however, that 'la vie associative' comprises a great variety of community groups which have preventive functions on an individual and on a societal level (see, for example, <u>L'Impatient</u> No.1, 1977, p.19). Public support for these and other organisations in the form of 'Centres de Service pour Associations' can of course also be used by self-help associations in health (cf. note 4). So also can they use the alternative media, i.e. many community papers, 'la presse associative' and 'free radios': one such has just been created especially for associations of the social sector (Espace 1901 Paris).

Self-help organisations

By this notion we refer mainly to acknowledged charities and voluntary organisations, often founded by parents of the handicapped but relying very much on professional care. Some of them run rather big institutions and many have lost a great deal of their original self-help character. Organisations of the chronically ill (diabetes, MS, etc.) - most of them being mainly pressure groups - seem to have developed later in France and in Germany alike. Overall, I doubt that there are large quantitative or qualitative differences between the two countries. But, at present, not enough is known about the exact size and activities of these organisations for a definite statement to be made. All that can be said is that this sector seems to be larger in France, because it is easier and more common for groups to become registered charities (association loi 1901 à but non lucratif).

Conclusion

The most obvious difference between France and Germany is the missing 'core' of self-help discussion groups in France. Instead there are 'groupes santé', which have just founded a national federation. These 'health groups' are difficult to locate in figure 1: they are partly founded by professionals and collaborate most of the time with them, but they call themselves groups of 'health users'. On the one hand they are close to the formal health care system because this is their most important point of reference, having such close ties with professionals, yet on the other hand they are remote from the formal health care system because they are very critical of its structures and institutions. They are action groups, though many of their activities ultimately mean discussion of specific health problems. They function as informal groups of equal users, but most of them are formally registered associations and would like to have paid staff. It is probably too daring to interpret these different developments only within a framework of a 'societal need' for self-help in all industrialised countries. But if one accepts this assumption, there seems to be a certain logic in the different developments.

One could take the Groupe Santé du 9e as an early and the most developed example of a typical health group as they are now being formed in many other places. This group has had a catalytic function for the formation of other self-help discussion groups. In Germany the formation of self-help discussion groups was strongly supported by interested professional helpers, the media and a growing number of researchers and politicians. Until now this support has been totally lacking in France. The 'groupes santé' are possibly a substitute for this lacking help. The users' movement has created, in the form of health groups, a tool, an 'infrastructure' for catalytic support, which is often helpful or even necessary for self-help groups to take off. The overwhelming reaction to this charter distributed by the newly founded National Federation has proved that there is a will in France to form groups and support all sorts of self-help activities.

Notes
(1) Further expressions which refer to at least part of the spectrum of self-help associations are: groupe (association) autogéré(e), auto-organisé(e), d'entraide, d'usagers, de malades, d'aide mutuelle. The notion 'groupes self-help' is very much identified with feminist groups (cf. Autrement, No.27/29, 1980). The boutiques de santé (health shops) are somewhat similar in their purposes to the British Community Health Councils. They are, however, not institutionalised as in England, and differ from the 'Gesundheitsladen' in Germany in that they have a stronger ambition to be users' groups, whereas the German health shops are all (but one) mainly a forum for medical and paramedical professionals. Users' associations are often very similar to the (French) health shops, but were mostly created as a sort of 'patient committee' by group practices that wanted to communicate with the local population they served. These two concepts are being abandoned in favour of groupes (de) santé. This seems to me the only French expression which is vague enough to cover all types of self-help associations.

(2) This would not have been possible without the help of those who were prepared to answer and discuss at length my questions (despite my poor mastery of the French language).

Amongst them, I am particularly grateful to Catherine et Liliane (Groupe Santé du 9e, Monique Minoux (Fédération Nationale des Groupes d'Usagers de la Santé), Annie-Claire Deyon (who works as a general practitioner in a Paris group practice and has edited a special issue of Pratiques on users' associations) and Serge Karsenty (former member of the Boutique de Santé du 10e and head of the research unit, Santé et Société). Despite their help my picture of the French health movement probably has many deficiencies. It is a view from outside and can only be understood as such. Serge Karsenty, to whom I am very grateful for comments on the first draft of this paper, did not completely agree with my rather optimistic view of the future development of self-help in France.

(3) See, for example, Nos. 11, 22 and 46 of L'Impatient. For a general overview of publications and innovations in health care covering the past ten years, see Giard et al (1980).

(4) Additional information on users' groups can be obtained from the Fédération Nationale d'Usagers de la Santé. I am also very much indebted to the kind staff of the Centre d'Information sur les Innovations Sociales. This centre provides excellent documentation on innovative approaches in health and other social fields as well as a guide for resource centres. (Guide pratique relatif aux Centres de Service pour Associations, 1980). The Association pour la Défense et l'Information sur la Santé also provides information for users, particularly with regard to the non-officially recognised therapy methods.

(5) For the first Boutique de Santé in Tours see Autrement, 1977, p.45. A general pciture of the Paris health shops is given by Perthuis (1980). The Boutique du 10e is described in Faire, June 1978. The Groupe Santé du 9e shares rooms with several other local groups (cf. Autrement, 1980, p.84). In the 11e arrondissement, the Association pour l'animation d'un centre de santé à Charonne has published its own journal, S comme Santé since March 1979.

(6) The Fédération Nationale d'Usagers de la Santé has started to produce a liaison bulletin for its members.

(7) See also the article by F. Bloch-Laine, (1981), the former president of the DAP. Newly registered associations relating to health are reported in Le Quotidien du Médecin.

(8) Another reason for the gap may be competition for financial support. The older organisations from the voluntary sector have comparatively fewer difficulties in getting funding from public institutions than the new health groups.

(9) 'Our' refers to the members of a research project on 'self-help groups in health: their origin, development, performance and effectiveness' (funded by the German Ministry of Research and Technology). I am very grateful to my colleagues in Hamburg

who took over my part of the work during my stay in Paris. I
would also like to thank the German Academic Exchange
Service and its staff in Paris for their help.

(10) I found most evidence of their existence in L'Impatient (see
No.45/46, 1981, p.15-18) and in Deyon (1979). After finishing
this article, I found further evidence for the similarity
between self-help groups in France and other European
countries during a visit to the 'Centre d'Etude et d'Information
sur le Volontariat'. I am very grateful to Jacqueline Couste,
who gave me some more information on the voluntary sector
in France, and drew my attention to a special issue of
Volontariat/Bénévolat No.11/12, 1980. This presented self-
help groups as a form of voluntary work and gave a list of
some fifty addresses of groups and organisations.

References and relevant literature

Alternatives(1978) 'Ressources Speciale', Alternatives, 6/7, Paris.

Autrement (1977) 'Francs-tireurs de la Médecine', Autrement, 9,
Paris

Autrement (1977) 'SMG, MAS ... et les enfants de 1968',
Autrement, Paris

Autrement (1980) 'La santé à bras le corps. De l'assistance à
l'autonomie, voyages au bout de la maladie', Autrement, 26,
Paris

Autrement (1980) 'Usagers et Santé. Rapport du colloque de
Rennes', Autrement, 27/29, Paris

Bloch-Laine, F. (1981) 'Le renouveau du mouvement associatif' in
J.D. Reynaud and Y. Grafmeyer (eds.) Francais, qui êtes-
vous?, La Documentation Francaise, Paris

Bruneau, C. and Rioux, J.P. (1981) Les associations en France 1930-
1980. Essai de bibliographie rétrospective, Institut d'Histoire
du Temps Présent, Paris

Busseau, J. (1980) 'Consommateurs de soins: les premiers pas',
Autrment, 26, Paris, 148-156

Clermont,P. (1981) 'Quand les groupes se régroupent', L'Impatient,
46, Paris, 3-5

Couste, J. (1981) 'Situation du Volontariat-Bénévolat en France',
Volonteurope: Occasional Paper, 1, Volunteer Centre,
Berkhamsted, 12-16

Deyon, A-C (1979) 'Les usagers comment se protènt-ils?',
Pratiques ou les cahiers de la médecine utopique, 33, Paris,
11-80

Dupuy, J.P. and Karsenty, S. (1974) 'L'Invasion Pharmaceutique',
Seuil, Paris

Giard, L. et al (eds.) (1980) Médecine, Santé et Usagers, 10, Group
de liaison pour l'action culturelle et scientifique, Paris

L'Impatient(1979) 'Desdocteurs sans cravate, le syndicat de la
médecine générale', L'Impatient, 16, Paris, 22-28.

L'Impatient (1982) 'Groupes Santé: voilà les GUS', L'Impatient, 50, Paris, 10-11.

Volontariat/Bénévolat (1980) 'Multiples Visages du Volontariat: Les groupes d'aide mutuelle', Volontariat/Bénévolat, 11/12, Paris, 3-6 Perthuis, C. (1980) 'Boutiques de Santé: l'autogestion à tâtons', Autrement, 26, Paris, 81-83

Pradal, H. (1974), Guide des médicaments les plus courants, Seuil, Paris

Pratiques ou les cahiers de la médecine utopique (1981), 'Pratiques nouvelles: Rêves et Réalités', Pratiques ou les cahiers de la médecine utopique, 48/49, Paris

Self-help Clearing House (1979) Self-help Spotlight, 11, Share Print Workshop, London.

Relevant addresses

L'Association pour la Défense et l'Information sur la Santé, 6, rue d'Andlau, 67300 Schiltigheim

Autrement, 4, rue d'Enghien, 74010, Paris

Centre d'Etude et d'Information sur la Volontariat, 130 rue des Poissoniers, 75018 Paris

Centre d'Information sur les Innovations Sociales, 18 rue de Varenne, 75007 Paris

Editions Alternatives et Parallèles, 6 rue des Bourdonnais, 75001 Paris

Fédération Nationale d'Usagers de la Santé, 5 bis, rue des Haudriettes, 75003 Paris

FONDA (Fondation pour la vie associative), 18 rue de Varenne, 75007 Paris

Groupe de liason pour l'action culturelle et scientifique, 20 rue Berbier du Mets, 75013 Paris

Institut d'Histoire du Temps Présent, 80 rue Lecourbe, 75015 Paris

L'Impatient, 9 rue Saulnier, 75009, Paris.

PART II PERSPECTIVES FOR PROFESSIONALS

SELF-HELP: A PSYCHOANALYST'S PERSPECTIVE
Kurt Buchinger

1. The notion of self-help works through two inter-related ideas contained within it. Firstly, it changes the shape of the relationship between the need for help and the giving of help. And secondly, it sees the dependence of one person upon another in a rather unusual way.

A. The relationship between the need for help and the giving of help

The difference between the two is usually understood in the form of a mutual contradiction. Either you need help, in which case you should seek to obtain it from someone who is competent to give it; or you are able to give help, in which case you are not allowed to be in need of that sort of help - at the very least you must have overcome your need for help, so that it does not interfere with your role as helper.

The separation of these two aspects reflects a fundamental, culturally rooted tendency to dissect an organic tension or contradiction into its component parts. There is something to be gained from this as long as it is done with an awareness of the intrinsic connectedness of the two elements. The particular characteristics of both aspects can then come fully into play. The need for help can unfold, it can be precisely analysed and better understood. Equally, the forms of helping can be developed, refined and in their particular fields of application can be identified. The interplay of both aspects becomes more differentiated and productive through division of labour and specialisation.

There is a danger concealed in this development. The more we emphasise the particular qualities of the two opposing aspects the more we lose sight of their intrinsic connectedness. We think we can observe the two aspects existing <u>separately</u>; in reality, we actually attribute them to different groups who then become, as we shall see, different classes of people: lay and professional, those needing help and those giving help.

This societal tendency is supported and partly explained by the psychic mechanisms involved in the splitting of ambivalences: we can either be active or passive, helpless or helping, masculine or feminine, powerful or powerless, competent or incompetent; but rarely both at the same time. The tension of the intrinsic

59

opposition is not easy to bear and we are inclined to transfer one of its elements outside of ourselves and attribute it to someone else, who is then supposed to manage it for us. The intrinsic opposition becomes an opposition between us and this other person.

With self-help there is no splitting, in the individual, of active and passive, help-needing and help-giving. Rather, both elements are united in every person. Self-help does not divide the person into two half-persons, as tends to happen in most relationships between professionals and lay people, and especially in the professional therapist-patient relationship.

Self-help does accept the difference between the need for help and the giving of help. However, it does not accept it in the form of a separation of the two aspects, a separation which lays the basis for a one-sided authority relationship in which each partner in the relationship embodies only one of the aspects. This brings us to the second thought that is important for the idea of self-help.

B. The dependence of one person on another

We tend to view the dependence of one person on another as one-sided, with an authority gradient that cannot be reversed. In so doing we are thinking in the unambiguous categories of super- and subordination. This is connected with our conditions of socialisation, taken in the widest sense. It has a psychogenetic explanation based on the experience of the infant and child as dependent on authority figures who ensure its physical and mental survival. This dependence is, of course, supposed to be overcome through individual maturation. However, there are interactional and institutional conditions of socialisation that stand in the way of that process, conditions which aid and abet a continuing infantilisation. Most of us spend most of our working lives - and hence most of our life - in hierarchically structured institutions, which take us back gently or not so gently to familiar stages of early childhood dependence. This tendency is not only supported by family interaction: the latter is also informed by it. Here we want to discuss the problems of dependence only in relation to the difference between the need for help and the giving of help, as specified in point A.

When anyone surrenders an important part of their person to another person and this is reciprocated, then these two people are dependent on each other. Half-people must, if they are to become whole again, enter into relationship with each other. But what does the relationship look like? It is a compulsive relationship in which they are both chained to each other, while remaining very much strangers to one another. For neither really regains from the other what has been surrendered - that part of one's own intrinsic contradiction that has been denied in oneself.

Since what is in fact involved is some part of us which none of us recognise in ourselves, the relationship necessarily becomes one-sided. Those who are only in need of help remain dependent on the help of others; those who are only givers of help depend on the helplessness of others. So there are doctors and patients, therapists and clients.

However, the denied part does not disappear: we all repress it in ourselves and continually encourage it in others. Patients in their helplessness want doctors to be more and more powerful; doctors, seeing themselves only as helpers, want patients to be more and more helpless. At the same time, we all promote our own admissible part and help it to hypertrophic growth. Doctors want themselves to be more and more powerful and helping, patients want themselves to be more and more helpless and incompetent. The one-sidedness and the authority gradient seem doubly secure: from inside and outside. Thus there arises in the compulsive relationship between the two an intrinsic dynamic, which tends to correspond to what Willi (1975) calls collusion: the active part must always become more active, the passive more passive, until both are overtaxed in their one-sidedness and the relationship becomes intolerable.

For the professional helping situation this means that methods of support become more and more professionalised, comprehensive and differentiated, and more and more obscure to the lay person. Lay people become less and less capable of giving one another the help needed and more and more dependent on the professions. This continues until aspects of the opposite become visible: patients make ever greater demands which make doctors aware of their own helplessness. Doctors consider patients to be less and less capable, until the latter refuse to accept this, discern the hidden helplessness of the doctors and rediscover their own capacities for self-help. Doctors make the same discovery. For them it is harder than it is for patients to encourage such developments because they stand to lose a privileged position in the one-sided relationship, while the patients leave behind an unprivileged, incapacitating position.

The concept of self-help overcomes the <u>one-sidedness</u> and the <u>authority gradient</u> in the dependence of one person upon another without denying the fundamental interdependence of people. Its conception of dependence is synonymous with a meaningful conception of autonomy: this has nothing to do with an isolated, single individual, but relates to a community of equal, mutually dependent persons. Self-help is, therefore, not the lonely affair of individuals striving to sort out by themselves the intrinsic opposition within them of the need for help and the capacity to help. The self-help movement is from the outset a group movement, in which the autonomy of the individual in relation to the problem, which was the reason for participation in the group, is achieved through and as the autonomy of the whole group.

2. How do these characteristics of self-help relate to the problem of mental health?

In my opinion, the work of self-help groups and organisations produces of itself therapeutic effects, without the involvement of theoretical knowledge of the mental and social origins of disorders or of technically highly developed professional therapeutic tricks. The two practical guiding principles discussed in A and B - the conception of the intrinsic union of the need for help and the capacity to help, and the conception of the equal autonomous dependence of people on one another - make group self-help as a whole a 'trick' that is simple for lay people and which is therefore of great therapeutic effect. For these principles are opposed to the most important originating conditions and functional mechanisms of psychosocial disorders. And to the extent that they are applied in the work of self-help groups and organisations, they overcome the effect of the functional mechanisms and the originating conditions of disorder. These claims will be explained below.

A. In the terms of a psychoanalytically orientated conflict theory, we can understand psychic disorders as the splitting of motives underlying our experience and behaviour, motives that belong together although they are often opposed to each other. We have already mentioned some of these oppositions and how the opposed parts are not allowed to appear together: we must not love and hate at the same time, at least not the same person; we must not be active and passive, at least not at the same time or for any length of time. A part of the motives that belong together is admissible and may enter our consciousness; we recognise ourselves as responsible for it, it lies within our competence, and we give it room to develop through upbringing, education and experience. Another part is not admitted by our conscious control over our feelings, and is pushed out of personal responsibility into the unconscious, where it remains preserved in its original undeveloped form. From there it releases uncontrolled archaic activity which, as an extraneous element, becomes intermixed with the admissible feelings in the form of symptoms.

The first mentioned practical principle of self-help is based on the overcoming of this splitting tendency that is fundamental to the maintenance of disorder; reconciling the helplessness that is experienced in relation to the disorder and one's own helping capacity that belongs with it, which the individual concerned cannot mobilise alone. Here, the second principle of self-help is important. The splitting tendency is overcome in a group of equals, people similarly affected by problems who, in their awareness of this situation, accept one another as belonging together. In their attempt at self-help they accept that they are dependent on one another. This fundamental solidarity makes it possible for them, in equal, autonomous, mutual dependence, to embrace together personal responsibility for something for which, until then, they had thought they had no responsibility, or which, until then, they could not cope with.

In this way, self-help achieves a twofold effect, which in professional psychotherapy (of the psychoanalytic variety, at least) can only be produced via a therapeutic regression, and even then only in part. Firstly, the overcoming of the afore-mentioned splitting encourages a readiness to overcome analogous splittings that lead to disorders. In developing this aspect of self-help work our ability to endure other intrinsic contradictions is increased. Unconscious split-off material finds it easier to enter our consciousness and is more easily accepted.

The second effect of self-help comes from fulfilling the self-help requirement of taking personal responsibility in the face of disorder. This relates not only to the helping activity but also to the concept of disorder. Self-help groups are neither presented with professional therapeutic methods nor given definitions of disorder. Self-help gives back to those affected the right not only to deal with their own problems but also to decide what should be viewed as disorder. There are self-help groups for psychosocial problems which do not appear in the official lists of psychic disorders, the so-called diagnostic schemata. Forms of behaviour which are listed as disorders are accepted by many self-help groups as 'normal' (Kickbusch and Trojan, 1981).

B. Psychic disorders can also be conceived in terms of unconquered one-sided dependencies. In these dependencies we find the reason for the psychological splitting of the experiential and behavioural motives that in fact belong together (as mentioned under A). There are various forms of one-sided dependencies which can make us mentally ill, by not recognising the claims of the dependent part to partial independence, and thereby only allowing it to come into its own in the form of disorders.

There are, first of all, intrapsychic one-sided dependencies, representing the processing of the external social dependencies to which we are exposed in the course of our psychogenesis. Instinctual desires and ego-needs, for example, which, when placed in one-sided dependence by the prohibitions of the superego, can find no satisfaction and then enforce their claims in the form of neurotic symptoms.

There are, secondly, one-sided interactional dependencies which, in a group of persons, as for example the family, lead to pathological consequences when they frustrate the claims of the members to independence and independent development. This claim is forced back in favour of the claims of the firmly established interactional system. The result is the threatening disturbance of the group equilibrium which can, for example, be explained away as the psychic disorder of a member (who then functions as the symptom carrier).

Thirdly, there are one-sided <u>institutional</u> dependencies, which are decisively involved in forming pathological interaction and intrapsychic structures. Thus, for example, the traditional, socially given role distribution promotes a denial and repression of important parts of the personalities of both parties. We are becoming increasingly aware of the fact that this arrangement results in the profound psychic and social subjection of those affected. It has destructive and pathological consequences both individually and in interaction, as well as in society as a whole. To give another example, the production of neurotic or psychosomatic symptoms, together with pathological personality changes, is encouraged by institutionally given roles at work, with their frequently fixed boundaries to psychic development and interaction.

Therapeutic efforts towards achieving psychic health attempt to transform the disabling one-sided dependencies into interdependencies by working on the manifold resistances that act against change. Thereby, as far as intrapsychic problems are concerned, instinctual claims and ego needs cease to be one-sidedly dependent on the superego; the latter, in their mature formation, become dependent on the former. In the case of interactional problems, not only is the scope for group members' experience and action to be defined by the group structure, but the latter is likewise affected by the changing or growing possibilities of the interacting persons. With regard to the institutional conditions, the identity-forming roles cease to be immutably and unquestionably given. Their particular forms are also capable of change by their occupants and of adaptation to new requirements.

Professional psychotherapy and counselling attempt to achieve this 'healing' transformation of one-sided dependencies into interdependencies, that is, into equal and mutual dependencies through a process in which the one-sided dependence of the client is therapeutically organised. The aim of this professional approach is to overcome the one-sided dependence of the client on professional methods or on the therapists and counsellors who advocate them. Frequently the question is posed, particularly about long-term forms of therapy using deep regression, as to whether one-sided therapeutic dependence does not have a socialising effect on the client extending in spite of deliberate efforts to the contrary, far beyond the end of therapy. It may well be that the resulting limitation of the possibilities for psychic health is not noticed because it corresponds to a general tendency, accepted as socially normal, to one-sided sub-and superordination.

With its principle of equal mutual dependence, which I have here equated with autonomy, self-help counteracts psychic disorders based on one-sided dependence. In this way it creates a climate that is conducive to the overcoming of disorders. The interdependence of participants in a self-help group contributes to

64

the overcoming of one-sided intrapsychic dependencies which are expressed in renewed social dependencies. In so doing, self-help also contributes towards transforming the latter into social interdependencies. Finally, self-help makes for the removal of institutional conditions conducive to disorder. It is itself an institution orientated towards the needs of its participants, freeing them from institutional dependency in the field of professional helping, without institutionalising new dependencies. It creates, in general, a new consciousness vis-a-vis institutional structures, issuing by its own example a challenge to the often disabling one-sided dependency on those structures.

C. **A qualifying observation.** I have spoken in the form of postulates about the two guiding practical principles of self-help and their effects in the field of mental illness and health. They are not a certificate of guarantee for practice. The latter must first be closely monitored to establish the extent to which it does justice to the two basic principles, or itself succumbs to splitting and dependency to which the idea of self-help is opposed. The postulates tell us little about which disorders can be remedied through self-help groups, and nothing about how fundamental such disorders might be. Detailed experience in self-help groups, together with considerable courage of an unconventional kind, are also necessary to answer these questions.

3. In conclusion, let us hazard the thesis that self-help makes a contribution to the problematic relationship between psychic disorder and guilt, by suggesting a new conception of the guilt capacity of the mentally ill. In this respect it stands in a long tradition of attempts at emancipation and carries it a significant step forward.

In medieval Christendom, mental illness was understood as a consequence and expression of guilt. In the context of a meaningful moral world order, it was the divinely decreed punishment and atonement for a sinful offence against that order. Hence, in a way, it was given a moral meaning itself. It was, however, a meaning which left people quite powerless, a meaning commanded by God alone according to his inscrutable ways. To those who, until then, had felt guiltless, the psychic illness that God imposed revealed the hidden guilt that they also bore. In that respect they were completely at its mercy and yet fully responsible for it - in other words, guilty. The awareness of a clear conscience was no defence against mental illness, which made it terrifyingly clear that people were estranged from themselves, not 'masters in their own house' as Freud was later to say. This connection of full responsibility and powerlessness with regard to psychic illness intensified the irrational guilt anxieties to an unbearable degree.

The modern scientific orientation and its triumph in psychiatry can be understood, among other things, as an attempt at liberation from this situation. Guilt anxieties were to be eliminated through the new conception of mental illness as a consequence of organic events. However, this approach did not break the connection between psychic disorder and guilt; it merely repressed it. In modern times, too, people were seen as fully responsible for meaningful psychic events. For this reason, therefore, psychic disorder had to be understood not as such but as a meaningless symptom of organic relationships, for which natural laws were solely responsible. That this denial of the psychic character of mental disorder represented a repression of its connection with guilt is shown by the return of the repressed in modern dealings with mental illness. Apart from generally delineating the latter, psychiatry still exhibits greater similarities with penal matters than with medicine. Until recently psychiatric institutions resembled prisons rather than hospitals, and many therapeutic measures had and have more of the character of punishments than of methods of treatment.

Furthermore, the medieval powerlessness of the individual was supposed to be turned into its opposite through the modern belief, orientated towards natural science, in the technical feasibility of everything. That this was a not quite successful defence becomes particularly clear in psychiatry. Here, medicine's promise to abolish suffering proved empty. The institutions became hidden places of custody, rather than places of treatment that were open to view. The one-sided dependence on the ways of God was indeed abolished, but in its place there came the dependence on the psychiatrist and his prescriptions.

It was only with the arrival of psychoanalysis that a further advance was made in the conquest of the connection between psychic illness and guilt. Its empirically and theoretically founded belief in the unconscious allows us to presume the existence of motives, which do indeed have a powerful effect on our experience and action, but which are beyond the reach of our conscious and responsible decisions. Psychoanalysis can, therefore, again understand psychic disorders as meaningful, motivated, emotional-mental events, and not as the meaningless consequences of organic processes, without ascribing to the patient full responsibility and moral guilt. It can also recognise that we do not rule in the house of our own psyche, without thereby surrendering us in one-sided dependence to the inscrutable ways of God or the psychiatrists. It does of course achieve its therapeutic effect through a long, fundamental and one-sided dependence of the client on the analyst. However, as already stated, that dependence is supposed to be methodically worked through and overcome in successful treatment.

With its replacement of one-sided dependence by the principle of mutual autonomous interdependence, self-help can move a step forward in this problem area. Whereas psychoanalysis has returned mental illness to the domain of meaningful psychic events, without allowing the connection between guilt and full responsibility to be revived, self-help achieves its successes while recognising our accountability for our disorders. In this way it can provide a new approach to the problem of our capacity for guilt, without evoking insurmountable guilt anxieties.

Self-help is able to raise the question of our guilt in relation to our disorders in a new way because it avoids blame and condemnation from outside. It is a case of guilt which can be recognised and jointly worked on through the solidarity of similarly affected persons who are not threatening one another. Guilt can thus once again be discussed as an aspect of autonomy and not in connection with one-sided dependence in which punishment is threatened.

4. These remarks are theses. By this I mean statements which in their one-sidedness invite contradiction. Perhaps the latter may complete and enrich rather than refute them. My wish is that they be read in that spirit.

References

Buchinger, K. (1981) 'Von der Einzeltherapie zur psychosozialen Selbsthilfe' (From individual therapy to psychosocial self-help) Psychosozial 4, pp.71-98.

Dorner, K. and Plog, U. (1978) Irren ist menschlich oder Lehrbuch der Psychiatrie/Psychotherapie (Mistakes are human or primer in psychiatry/psychotherapy), Psychiatrie Verlag, Wunstorf.

Illich, I. et al (1978) Entmundigung durch Experten (Infantilised by experts), rororo.

Katz, A.H. and Bender, E.I. (eds.) (1976) The strength in us: Self-help groups in the modern world. Franklin Watts, New York.

Kickbusch, I. and Trojan, A. (1981) Gemeinsam sind wir starker (Together we are stronger), Fischer alternativ, Frankfurt.

Moeller, M.L. (1978) Selbsthilfegruppen (Self-help groups), Rowohlt, Hamburg.

Moeller, M.L. (1981) Anders helfen: Selbsthilfegruppen und Fachleute arbeiten zusammen (A different way to help: Self-help groups and professionals work together), Klett-Cotta, Stuttgart.

Richter, H.E. (1978) 'Psychoanalyse und psychosoziale Therapie' (Psychoanalysis and psychosocial therapy), Psychosozial, 1, pp.7-29.

Willi, J. (1975) Die Zweierbeziehung (Two person relationships), Rowohlt, Hamburg.

SELF-HELP AND THE MEDICAL PRACTITIONER
Michael L. Moeller

Looking back over the last decade, the New York Times of 1 January 1980 characterised the seventies as the decade of self-help groups. These groups have already ushered in a silent revolution in medical care. Throughout the western industrial nations, several hundred thousand independent 'talking' groups have sprung up. In a recent publication, four hundred and fifty different organisations are described (Moeller, 1981). There is no illness or psycho-social affliction against which self-help groups cannot be of use. Why they are an invaluable addition to medical practice, how the doctor can collaborate with them and what difficulties and successes they have, will be briefly outlined in what follows.

The second German General Practitioners' Day 1979 devoted a three-hour panel discussion to a theme that has become topical: General Practitioners, Self-help Groups and the Medical System. A specialist in internal medicine from Bremen reported that in his practice he was already collaborating with seven self-help groups. Does the collaboration of general practitioners with self-help groups figure among the essential future tasks of medical activity? In all probability, yes.

The great successes of scientific medicine have given rise to an almost unmanageable new demand; chronically sick and disabled people who, through technical help, are saved from early death, now also expect medical assistance to help them cope with the accompanying long-term psycho-social stresses and the often far-reaching family and occupational adjustments.

For practitioners, the close relationship between sickness and recovery and the living conditions, behaviour and attitudes of their patients remains the easiest approach. However, doctors are aware that technical medicine must be complemented by personal medicine. We help a fat patient not just with dietary advice; nor a diabetic with information alone, however conscientiously we give it; nor someone suffering from high blood pressure just with orders for regular check-ups; nor a heart infarct patient only with exhortations to adopt a relaxed lifestyle. What is missing here, and in countless other cases, is the chance to perceive with greater awareness one's own behaviour and everyday life and to make more lasting changes in them.

This is precisely what is offered by those self-help groups which, as self-accountable talking groups, set themselves the task of working through their own problems together. Here, the association of medical practice and self-help groups offers a great opportunity for a deeper doctor-patient relationship, which can have helpful effects where the limited individual medical consultation is insufficient. No longer does the doctor (or the patient) need to feel as helpless as before, when faced with those multifarious psycho-social conflicts, which appear in the consult-ation in the form of aggravated physical complaints. Whether preventative (as in the case of functional disorders), curative (as with obesity), or rehabilitative (as, for example, following an operation for cancer), self-help groups can be seen as simple, basic psychological therapy. They cannot, of course, replace medical measures, but they can provide an excellent complementary approach. They are indicated for all manifest or latent psycho-social stress, be it consequence, concomitant condition or additional cause of the illness.

Objective: to arouse the therapeutic capacities of the participants
In a self-help group six to twelve persons meet together. In regular discussion they learn, without the collaboration of a therapist, how to deal with their conflicts in a more appropriate manner, and they try to resolve their emotional problems together. They meet once a week for several years, in sessions lasting about two or three hours in a room that is as neutral as possible.
The most important characteristics of group self-treatment are
- all group members are of equal status;
- each member decides for himself or herself;
- the group is responsible for its own decisions;
- each member joins the group because of his/her own difficulties;
- what is discussed in the group is to remain within the group and is not for outside consumption (group obligation of confidentiality);
- participation in the group is free.
The aim of participation in a self-help group is to help oneself and others through intensive discussion of personal problems, of whatever sort, and through grappling with the feelings that arise. Experiences in groups and scientific investigations have shown that this goal is achievable. Everyone has therapeutic abilities, and uses them in everyday life, being able to apply them more or less well according to the situation. The self-help group offers a particularly good opportunity to awaken these capacities and to put them to good effect.
Every self-help group goes through different phases. Initial anxieties and lack of trust are overcome through the fact that all the members bring with them into the group their reservations, feelings and conflicts. In time, with regular sessions, a strong group feeling develops even if some members leave and new people

join. Experience shows that every group finds its own style of working together. Special rules are not necessary. Group self-treatment is a process of growing personal self-discovery. One gains insight into previously unsuspected connections in one's life and in one's problems.

Not all groups have a medico-psychological orientation

Besides these independent psycho-social discussion groups, we can distinguish six other sorts of self-help groups. First, there are the medical self-help groups, like the rheumatics association, women's post-cancer self-help groups and a further 28 associations in the Federal consortium 'Hilfe fur Behinderte' (Help for handicapped people), with over a quarter of a million members. These mainly confine themselves to 'external' self-help (legal and social advice, promotion of research and legislative lobbying). Secondly, there are the consciousness changing self-help groups like the groups in the women's liberation movement, or homosexual groups. Thirdly, there are the life-forming self-help groups which include, among others, residential and rural communes. Fourthly, there are work-orientated self-help groups in which young people and older unemployed people have come together in order to find themselves an occupational activity. There is also an ever-growing development of training-orientated self-help groups, for example for nurses, social workers and psychotherapists, representing self-organised further training. Finally, there are the community action groups which should all be counted as self-help groups.

For the establishment of groups the doctor provides encouragement only

In answer to the question of how self-help groups can arise in the context of medical practice there are no hard and fast rules, only suggestions. Different doctors will find their own approach and their own style. Starting from scratch it would be necessary to talk personally with just a few patients and to encourage the formation of self-organised groups. Two or three patients, together with the doctor as an equal-ranking counsellor, should then find enough people to form a group. To begin with this can be done by means of a notice in the waiting room. A small, typed sheet of paper is sufficient, with a text roughly as follows: 'Interested in exchanging experiences on a regular basis in an independent discussion group? We meet ... (time and place). If you'd like to find out more please contact ... (contact person and doctor)'.

Leaflets are also very helpful and can be left in the waiting room or given out by the doctor or the paramedical staff. Leaflets of this sort with general or particular information, can be obtained free of charge from the Deutschen Arbeitsgemeinschaft Selbsthilfegruppen (German working party on self-help groups). Wherever possible a contact address, as well as a definite place and a regular time, should be arranged before the establishment of the group. Through talking on a one-to-one basis with people in similar situations, one's fear of others is frequently dissolved more easily than by the doctor's persuasion.

If the practice can provide a fairly large room for evening meetings which is acceptable to those involved, this should be made known through the notice in the waiting room. In the panel discussion on self-help groups at the GPs' Day mentioned above, the waiting room was already transformed into a regular contact and group meeting room. When the first groups have been set up, where possible new people should not go directly to the self-help group meetings but to the monthly joint meeting (see below). In my book, 'Selbsthilfegruppen' (Self-help groups) (1978) I have gone into all the practical questions in detail, and have included a chapter on setting up groups (pp.159-202).

The doctor as fellow counsellor on an equal footing
There are two tasks in particular that doctors can perform:
-     in the medical consultation, as a link person with the self-help groups;
-     in the joint group meeting, as a counsellor for self-help groups.

First of all, it is essential to emphasise the independence and self-responsibility of the prospective group participants; there can be no referral to the self-help group. It is necessary for the doctor, during the medical consultation, to draw the patient's attention to the, as yet little known, form of self-help in independent groups. The patient should make his own decision. In the self-help groups he no longer has the role of patient. He must ultimately decide for himself whether joining a group is useful. If people find a self-help group useful they will normally remain in it.

The doctor's task would be:
-     to point out the possibility and therapeutic potential of self-help groups;
-     to draw attention to the acclimatisation period of about ten sessions, and to reach an understanding with the patient that only after this can he make a well-founded decision;
-     to discuss all the feelings of ambivalence and anxiety that patients experience, which make their decision more difficult. These usually centre on a number of anxieties (see below).

As counsellor with the self-help groups the doctor takes part in the monthly joint meetings. It is important to pay careful attention to the equality of the relationship as opposed to the traditional patient-doctor dependency. The doctor should not counsel the groups, but counsel with them.

Monthly joint meetings of all groups help to solve common problems

In the joint sessions several self-help groups meet together to exchange experiences and to consult on matters of common concern. The joint meeting is, so to speak, 'the self-help group of the self-help groups'. Wherever possible all participants should attend; in practice that is rarely possible. As a rule the two-hour session is held once a month. Longer intervals are not conducive to mutual counselling. The exchange of experience takes place in the form of an open discussion. The significance of the joint meeting lies in the enrichment of the self-help group work, in the exploration of problems that a group finds hard to cope with, and in preventing the premature break-up of groups.

The joint meeting pursues several aims: the first and most important task area is the mutual exchange of experience concerning the progress of the self-help group work. The main interest is the lively description of what is happening in the groups. The individual groups are thus able to see beyond their own circle and can learn from one another. Discussion should focus not so much on personal problems (which should be dealt with in the particular self-help group) but on problems of the group as a whole. New people can come to the joint meeting, talk with experienced participants and either join an existing group or even form a new one.

In the joint meeting groups can also try to introduce useful social changes. For example, a self-help group for future parents could recommend rooming-in in clinics and hospitals.

Day-to-day common tasks and problems of self-organisation are dealt with by the participants in the joint meeting (notices, room bookings, etc.). The joint meeting also develops new ideas for the self-help groups, perhaps reciprocal observation visits by two such groups, larger weekend meetings, etc.

The doctor or other specialists can take part in the joint meetings. In this situation they are not therapists but self-help group counsellors; they prescribe nothing, but make their knowledge freely available.

Where necessary, in the initial period, the joint meeting can be run by a single group. It sets itself the goal of exploring its own group process from outside, as it were, and consults with the doctor on medical questions. The relative inexperience of most doctors with regard to group processes has its advantages: it reduces the danger that they might steer the group too much. The special function of the doctor is that of a catalyst or stabiliser. Experience shows that the doctor's presence, in itself, has the effect of being a useful crystallising nucleus for the exchange of experience. The doctor participates less as an expert and more as an 'ordinary' person.

The extent to which this activity which has been carried out by doctors without charge can be remunerated, remains to be seen. In the existing system of scale charges, a solution will surely be found to this problem. The new role of the doctor and the issues connected with possible payment - for example, an undesirable increase in patient dependency - are dealt with in more detail in my book, 'Anders helfen: Selbsthilfegruppen und Fachleute arbeiten zusammen' (Helping in other ways: Self-help groups and professionals work together) (1981). This is of relevance to all members of the helping professions.

Anxieties that arise must be dealt with by medical consultation

In a sense the doctor acts as a gate-keeper for numerous threshold anxieties. The anxieties appear in various garb from slight discomfort or transparent excuses to firm conviction. In this connection, doctors are no exception. On the basis of many years' experience the following points can be made.

Reservations about self-help: the idea of working as equals and without a leader contradicts a widespread, deep-rooted need for guidance, as well as the accustomed passive role of the patient. Independent groups are therefore regarded with scepticism - not only by lay people, but perhaps especially by those who are professionally involved in helping and educating. Many people cannot see that self-help groups have been proved to work successfully.

Fear of personal change: this relates to the fear of the indefinite, the unknown, the new. It is linked to anxiety about one's own conflicts but seems to be about something else. To change accustomed behaviour, to evaluate one's whole situation differently, to give up familiar feelings about oneself and one's awareness of life - all this is experienced as uncomfortable or even threatening.

Nervousness in the group: most people have no idea of the way in which personal, very private problems can be expressed in a group, although group treatment by therapists has for decades been a normal part of proven psychotherapeutic methods.

Fear of others: this is one of the most universal and basic of all human fears. Most people have not yet experienced how quickly it gives way to an intense feeling of closeness in the group.

Fear of one's own problems: no one enjoys meeting his own difficulties and weaknesses. This constitutes the well-known resistance observed during any psycho-therapy. On the other hand, one cannot resolve conflicts by constantly avoiding them. But this problem is quickly alleviated when it is seen in the group that no-one is without serious conflicts and that all are in the same boat.

Fear of damage to reputation: many people are beset by the fear that outsiders might look askance at them if they join a group. So they allow themselves to be influenced by the opinions of others.

A much greater cause for concern is the belief in the positively dangerous idea that health is synonymous with absence of conflict. On the contrary, health is based on <u>conflict capacity</u>. It is precisely this capacity to become aware of conflicts and to cope better with them that is developed in every good self-help group. <u>Fear of feeling hurt because one cannot cope on one's own</u>: finally, the fact that the group can do more than the individual usually means an unadmitted, anxiety-creating injury for convinced loners and individualists who are very much the product of increasing social isolation and modern meritocracy. There is still widespread currency for the erroneous conception that the healthy person can and must manage everything alone. The uninhibited exchange with others, that is, the capacity for group life, is an essential characteristic of emotional health; this truth has almost sunk into oblivion.

The seven fears listed above usually form the main background for the explanatory discussion with the doctor.

Inner resistance in the early sessions is normal

For an accompanying counselling service it is useful to be aware of some of the main difficulties encountered by self-help groups. Starting anything is difficult. In the first ten sessions every new person is shy with strangers. The others are still an unknown quantity and sometimes even unlikeable. Often, with plenty of excuses or even apparent conviction, new members want to stop attending group meetings. For this reason it is especially important to recommend attendance at the first ten sessions, come what may, not allowing oneself to be put off by annoying experiences like feeling uncomfortable, anxious, or a lack of trust, etc. After this initial period one should be able to make a clear decision as to whether or not one would like to remain a member of the group.

Experience shows that the group should, above all, make clear arrangements. The group should not be more than twelve or less than six in number. Regular participation is very important. It is also important not to lose sight of the aim of discussing personal concerns in the group. Again and again groups leave too many things undetermined: the best crew can do nothing if the boat they share is not watertight.

The best situation is when people are ready to risk expressing to the group the feelings that arise in them as openly as possible. It is particularly difficult to express so-called negative feelings, since they are strongly repressed in everyday life: dislike, anger, shame, envy, hurt, etc. However, these are precisely the feelings that are important for the progress of the whole group. Real affection can only develop when these negative feelings·are also openly explored.

Finally, the main resistance shown to a self-help group is simply to stay away. Since staying away can also be the result of participants themselves deciding that attendance is not useful in their case, there must be careful exploration of dropping-out by those affected and by the counsellor. It is then usually possible to throw some light on the circumstances. Clarification is worthwhile because, unfortunately, it is precisely when essential problems are involved that resistance increases.

Better relations with oneself and with others

The growth and differentiation of self-help groups are a sign of their effectiveness. There is no reason for staying in a group other than the fact that it is helpful. Empirical investigations show that self-help groups lead to major therapeutic changes (Daum and Moeller, forthcoming, Moeller and Daum, forthcoming; Stulinger, 1977). During the first three months of participation, as a rule, there do not appear to be any improvements. After six months, sociability increases. This is the first precondition for dealing better with one's own problems. After a year almost everyone feels healthier. The main results are a decline in depressive tendencies, a reduction in physical and emotional complaints, an increase in the capacity to make relationships, and greater readiness and ability to help others.

In more general terms, those involved learn anew how to talk with other people about essential matters, how to open up and, not least, how to listen as well. Knowledge of people and experience of life are widened. Dealing with one's own disorders becomes more successful. Most people stay in the group for two years.

The collaboration of doctors with patients who take responsibility for themselves introduces a new doctor-patient relationship. This goes beyond the traditional relationship of dependence and can be understood as the emancipation of the helping relationship. If successful medicine is to be understood as help towards self-help, then here we are dealing with a particularly effective form, namely, help towards group self-help. Thus, the ancient Hippocratic principle is fulfilled in a modern way, as it were; 'the doctor is only the helper, the patient himself, however, is the doctor'.

References

Daum, K.W. and Moeller, M.L. (forthcoming) Therapieerfolge bei Selfsthilfegruppen. Eine empirische Untersuchung an sechs Selbsthilfegruppen (Therapeutic success in self-help groups. An empirical investigation based on six self-help groups).

Moeller, M.L. (1978) Selbsthilfegruppen (Self-help groups). Rowohlt, Reinbek/Hamburg.

Moeller, M.L. (1981) Anders helfen: Selbsthilfegruppen und Fachleute arbeiten zusammen (A different way to help: Self-help groups and professionals work together). Klett-Cotta, Stuttgart.

Moeller, M.L. and Daum K.W. (forthcoming) Veranderungen wahrend der Teilnahme an einer Selbsthilfegruppe: Eine empirische Untersuchung an sechs Selbsthilfegruppen (Changes during participation in a self-help group: an empirical investigation based on six self-help groups).

Stubinger, D. (1977) 'Psychotherapeutische Selbsthilfegruppen in der Bundesrepublik. Eine Untersuchung uber Sozialstruktur und therapeutische Prozesse in den Gruppen'. Med. Inaug. Diss. (Psychotherapeutic self-help groups in the Federal Republic of Germany: an investigation into social structure and therapeutic processes in the group. Medical thesis). University of Giessen.

More information can be found in the two books written by this author (referred to above) or from the Deutsche Arbeitsgemeinschaft Selbsthilfegruppen (German working party on self-help groups), Friedrichstrasse 28, D-6300, Giessen, Germany. An earlier version of this article appeared in Medizinische Klinik, 76 (1981).

SELF-HELP AND MEDICAL EDUCATION
M. Bremer Schulte

The WHO goal of attaining 'health for all by the year 2000' - in accordance with the slogan from the Alma Ata conference - raises a number of questions. One of these concerns the function of medical faculties in implementing programmes that include a new emphasis on health promotion, disease prevention and supportive health education, especially on self-help and self-care. In conventional medical education there has been little or no interest in systematically facilitating or promoting an awareness of patients themselves as effective resources in health care. Patients themselves have not been considered active participants in their own health care. However, the medical practitioner of the present decade needs insight and understanding of the political and economic context of patient initiatives and self-care practices, as well as sensitivity towards these aspects of health care. This demands special know-how and other skills which have to be used in conjunction with clinical knowledge.

In this article one aspect of this broad topic will be elaborated, namely the attention devoted in medical education to:
-   self-activity and problem-solving by the people themselves; and
-   the corresponding role of professionals in health care, in this case physicians.

The term 'self-activity of patients' is used in the sense of self-activity of people in relation to their own health, covering self-care, participation in self-help groups and health promoting activities in general. The development of 'self-activity of patients and a corresponding role for physicians' is considered to be an objective of the health system in general, not specifically restricted to basic, primary or secondary care.

The objective of this contribution is to argue for more attention to this theme in medical curricula. This will be done by reporting research data from a project concerning counselling of and by chronically ill and handicapped persons, called 'patient counselling and patient organisation' (PAGO) and by analysing the programme of the medical faculty of the State University of Limburg.

Various studies (Brouwer, 1980; Council of Europe, 1979; Levin, 1976; Strauss, 1975) suggest that for those who suffer from a chronic disease (diabetes, asthma, coronary heart disease,

77

epilepsy, migraine, etc.), constituting at least 75 per cent of the current morbidity in developed countries, the conscious participation of the patient in his own care is essential to the realisation of even narrowly viewed clinical goals. Deeper understanding and adoption of an appropriate diet, medication, physical exercise, rest and other everyday routines require above all an effective level of interchange and co-operation between the physician and the patient. Such co-operation frequently requires the understanding and help of persons in the immediate environment who are important to the patient, such as his partner/spouse.

Many factors have led to an urgent questioning in many quarters of the effectiveness of health care and the scale of resources to be allocated to it in future. This article seeks to demonstrate that:

- this unprecedented questioning ought to influence the content of medical education;
- the reallocation of decreasing financial resources is necessary and should result in more money for research, leading to more insights into the possibilities and limitations of self-activity with regard to one's own health.

Our research is concerned with the field between the professional and the self-help/self-care part of the health system, as visualised in the equilibrium model portrayed in the diagram below.

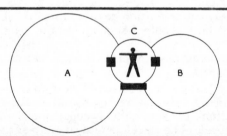

The term health system is used for the institutional professional health care (A) plus the field of self-care/self-help/mutual aid among peers (B). The latter is the mutual caring which has always existed everywhere among citizens and which is increasing with the spread of patients' organisations. Our studies concern the field in between (C), where the complementarity and possibilities as well as the restrictions of the interaction and co-operation between (A) and (B) can be explored, analysed and elaborated.

The resolution of the Council of Europe on the patient as an active participant in his own treatment includes the following recommendations on professional education and training:

Health policies and practices whereby professionals will come to perceive it as their responsibility to encourage the active participation of the patient in his own treatment should be promoted. In this respect, professionals should be discouraged from taking over people's responsibility for their own health, self-help capacities and rehabilitation

Innovations in the education of health care agents, which aim at attitude development enabling professionals to be receptive to the patients' needs and to facilitate the patients' co-operation in their own treatment, should be promoted.

Training curricula for students and all professionals which are geared to society's need for improvement of primary health care should envisage the earliest possible contact with practice in primary health care and the psycho-social problems of the patients involved. Subsequent and vocational training should be integrated and related to practice, not only with hospital patients, but also with patients in first line care. This should include appropriate training in prevention, prophylaxis, early diagnosis and health education. This will prepare them for future co-operation in health care terms. (Council of Europe, 1979)

A general basis for inputs into the medical curriculum at the State University of Limburg is provided by research projects of the faculty. This type of input is considered particularly necessary in innovative fields. In the medical curriculum data from two projects are used to introduce the broad field of self-activity methods in the health system and the corresponding consequences for the role of doctors in the 1980s.

The Psoriasis project

The target of this project consisted of people with a chronic skin disease, viz. psoriasis. This disease is believed to have a prevalence in the Netherlands of 2.5 per cent. The psoriasis patients who took part in the project came together for group treatment in twelve sessions over a period of three months. What took place in the groups with psoriasis patients and their partners is described elsewhere (Bremer Schulte et al, 1982).

A fellow patient functioned as their co-helper together with a professional as co-worker, according to what is called the duo-formula. Before adopting these roles they were trained together as a duo. The patient in the duo is called the co-helper, meaning by this that he helps fellow patients suffering from the same illness. The professional in the duo is called the co-worker, meaning by this that he is no longer the traditional expert who prescribes, but far more the facilitator or deliverer of service, putting his insight and skills at the patients' disposal and adding his expertise to the patients' experience.

Data for quantitative analysis were collected through a questionnaire. A pre-test post-test control group design was used. In comparison with a control group the experimental groups showed changes in the dimensions examined in the desired direction, notably a decrease of illness behaviour, an increase of social behaviour, an increase of contacts, an openness to other points of view and an increase in problem-solving capacities.

Whereas originally the psycho-social aspects of the disease were the main preoccupation, in the course of the project the need for an integrated approach to somatic and psycho-social aspects became more and more evident. The need to train duos of dermatologists and co-helpers for group treatment by and for persons with a chronic skin disease, together with their partners, was one of the conclusions and recommendations resulting from this investigation.

In discussion of the effects and the process of this experiment the relationship between experiential and professional expertise is clarified with the help of the equilibrium model described earlier. The intention is to contribute to the theoretical framework of planned change in health care. Attention is paid to the significance of such a project, not only for health care and research, but also for medical education. The significance of the results of this study for the training of general physicians and of dermatologists gradually becomes clear. A replication of the project has been designed as part of the training of the latter.

Reintegration with duos

The second pilot study, subsidised by the Dutch Heart Foundation, was designed on the basis of the first one. Reintegration refers to the process of healing with regard to the emotional as well as the physical consequences of myocardial infarction. With duos means that group-centred after-care is offered to post myocardial infarction patients and their partners by a couple comprising a fellow patient/co-helper who has passed through a heart infarction and a health care professional/co-worker, who are trained together. In this pilot study, the health care professionals were mostly general practitioners.

During group meetings the participants learned to measure their pulse rate and blood pressure and, in order to be able to render mutual aid in crisis situations, they also learned mouth to mouth resuscitation and cardiac massage. The object was to make the patients and their partners less uncertain and anxious. In addition, the participants were helped to recover from emotional shock by learning to eliminate excessive apprehension and to regain their former rhythm of life as far as desirable.

A controlled experiment was conducted with six groups of myocardial infarction patients and their partners. Once a week they had a meeting with a duo. These meetings lasted about one and a half hours. It was hypothesised that particular aspects of an illness would generally have a less negative impact on physiological and behavioural health outcomes in proportion to the extent that they were perceived to be manageable. Besides quantitative analysis through a self-reporting questionnaire, qualitative methods were used with a view to increasing the reliability of interpretation. The outcome of measurements in the experimental group was compared with that of a control group of myocardial infarction patients and their partners who had not yet participated. The experimental group consisted of 58 first mycocardial infarction patients plus their partners and the control group of 31. Allocation between the two groups was randomised.

The resulting data showed the following differences in favour of the experimental group:

- a decrease in the patients' anxiety and also in that of their partners;
- an increase in the ability to measure their pulse rate and blood pressure and carry out mouth to mouth resuscitation and cardiac massage;
- a decrease in illness behaviour of the patients as well as a decrease in their reaction to this behaviour by their partners;
- a decrease in depressive feelings.

The qualitative analysis showed evidence of better relationships between patients and their partners, including those relating to sexual contact; of a decrease in feelings of anxiety and uncertainty as the first aid skills were mastered; of the essential role of the duo who led the groups; and of the equal importance of both members of the duo.

Thus group-centred after-care seems to fulfil a genuine need on the part of the patients. Reintegration with duos deserves a place in health care. A replication of this study on a larger scale is in progress, which will measure somatic risk factors more systematically than in the first one. Both studies support the view that patients can be more active in handling their own health problems, and that professional and institutional care can support and stimulate self-care by acting in a facilitating way, rather than functioning in the conventional more directive and prescriptive manner.

The medical curriculum at the State University of Limburg

Since its establishment in 1974 the Faculty of Medicine at the State University of Limburg has chosen to focus especially on teaching and research in primary health care. The justification for this eighth medical school in Holland lies, among other things, in the possibility that it could experiment with the form and content of medical education. It is an illusion to think that medical students will ever get more than a fragmentary knowledge of the medical science at their disposal. Hence students must obtain the skills to solve medical problems for themselves with the help of modern aids. The image of the physician as the medical know-all authority belongs to the past. The patient wants information about his situation and about alternative possibilities for treatment. As a result a different kind of training is required. The intention is to respond to the changing needs of the health system in the Netherlands by focussing the programme on primary health care. Preventive medicine, sociological and psychological determinants of health and multi-disciplinary team work are given special attention.

The following educational principles are embodied in the basic philosophy of the medical faculty: problem-oriented learning, self-activity, continuous evaluation and attitude development. The curriculum is designed to cover the problem areas of primary health care, rather than to embody a strict framework of basic and adjunct disciplines. Students are confronted in the first four years mostly with the kind of problems occurring in the daily practice of the primary care physician. In the last two years the accent lies more on practical training, not only in the different departments of the general hospital but also in general practice and first line and mental health care.

As to self-activity of students as a central educational principle: there are hardly any lectures. Students must study what they need to know in the context of each problem. Collaboration with fellow-students on the problems presented is another basic theme. Students are randomly allocated into groups of eight, each group with a staff member as tutor. He is responsible for promoting the group's learning process as a whole rather than a particular discipline. This small group method provides supervision of the effort and progress of each student, and at the same time gives experience in team work and small group work. The curriculum is divided into blocks of six weeks' duration. In each block one central theme is treated. The problems treated during a block are presented in block books. References are made to relevant literature and the problems are presented in different theoretical and practical contexts. These lead to different resources, such as consultations with experts in specific fields and individual and group training in the skills laboratory. Here approximately two hundred medical and social skills are taught, ranging from basic measuring skills and training with simulated patients, to interviewing, physical examination and basic treatment procedures. The students gradually get acquainted with day to day health care practice by connecting the problems and training covered in the block books and tutorial groups with real health care procedures.

The curriculum structure for the first four years is given in Table 1.

Table 1: Curriculum for the first four years

First year of the course	Intro-duction to the study of medicine	Traumata	Infections	Psycho-somatic reactions	Athero-sclerosis	Oncology
Second year	Embryo & fetus	The child	The adolescent	The grown-up	The elderly person	Optional training
Third year	Fever & inflamm-ation	Fatigue	Shortness of breath & pain in the chest	Life styles		Optional training
Fourth year	Abdomi-nal com-plaints	Disturb-ances of menses & complic-ations in pregnancy	Headaches unconsc-iousness & neuro-logical/psych-iatric problems	Backaches & pain of the extr-emities		Optional training

The first year of the programme is devoted to an introduction and orientation to medicine and medical care. The second year covers the study of the healthy individual in relation to his physical and social environment. In the third and fourth years the various complaints most frequently faced in first-line care provide the starting points for further study. In the last two years students are placed as assistants in hospitals, general practices and psychiatric clinics, partly on an elective basis.

Evaluation of the programme
The 1980-81 programme for the first four years of the curriculum has been evaluated in the light of the central concern of this article. The question is whether the faculty is focusing on primary health care in teaching and research in such a way that self-activity of the patient gets the attention of the students and leads them to collect information and develop the attitudes and skills to enhance it. The nineteen block books for the first four years have been reviewed in relation to the following questions:

1. Where is the self-activity of patients explicitly included in the programme, in which form (F) and in what content (C)?
2. Where it is missing, what supplements are needed (S)?

These questions have been answered by making an inventory, carried out independently with three judges. The outcome has been discussed with each of the block co-ordinators. Table 2 reviews each theme with regard to form (F), content (C) and supplemental places (S).

Table 2: Presence of self-activity of patients in the block-books of the first four years, indicated with Form (F), Content(C) or Supplemental places(S)

First year of the course	Intro-duction to the study of medicine	Trau-mata	Infections	Psycho-somatic reactions	Athero-sclerosis	Oncology
		(2S)		(F-2S)	(F-S)	(S)
Second year	Embryo & fetus	The child	The adolescent	The grown-up	The elderly person	Optional training
	(F-2C)	(S)	(3F-S)	(S)	(3C-S)	
Third year	Fever & inflamm-ation	Fatigue	Shortness of breath & pain in the chest	Life styles		Optional training
		(F)	(F)	(2F)		
Fourth year	Abdomi-nal com-plaints	Disturb-ances of menses & comp-lications in pregnan-cy	Headaches unconsc-iousness & neuro-logical/ psych-iatric problems	Backaches & pain of the extr-emities		Optional training
	(3F-S)	(F)	(C-F)	(3F)		

The F places are elucidated in Table 3 with short comments.

Table 3:   Presence of self-activity in form (F)

Year Block		Form-indications (F)
1.1	Intro. to medicine	-
1.2	Traumata	-
1.3	Infections	-
1.4	Psychosomatic	Adolescent with life-problems referred to primary network factors.
1.5	Atherosclerosis	Man after m.c. infarction stimulated to investigate stress in the working situation.
1.6	Oncology	-
2.1	Embryo and foetus	Care of mammae during pregnancy
2.2	The child	-
2.3	The adolescent	Consequences of back-deterioration for work and profession Self-treatment of skin deficiencies (acne) Psychogenic complaints of impotence
2.4	The grown-up	-
2.5	The elderly	-
3.1	Fever & infection	-
3.2	Fatigue	Psychogenic fatigue
3.3	Shortness of breath	Instruction on self-care for a man who has to abandon pigeon-fancying because of lung complaints
3.4	Life styles	Advice on physical training by the GP Problem of a fat woman Handling stress
4.1	Abdominal complaints	Person with jaundice learns to regulate his rest and food Motivation of a patient with ulcus ventriculi to decrease smoking Stimulation of a patient to fast because of salmonella poisoning
4.2	Menses/pregnancy	Guidance of a pregnant woman to stop smoking

4.3	Neurol./psych- iatric problems	Guidance of a patient with epilepsy
4/4	Backaches	Therapy and exercise for a patient with rheumatoid arthritis Slimming for a fat woman with joint complaints Guidance of a man with runner's fracture to change his training scheme

A survey of C places with suggestions for supplements follows in Table 4.

Table 4: <u>Presence of self-activity in the content (C) and suggestions for supplements (S)</u>

Year& Block	Content indications (C)	Suggestions for supplements (S)
1.1	-	(After-care for myocardial infarction patients)
1.2	-	(Barbecue burning) guidance for people with severe scars; death of a child in the family: guidance during mourning processes
1.3	-	-
1.4	-	Self-activity essential in cases of all psychosomatic diseases; self-help and self-care for people with hyperventilation and asthma
1.5	-	Motivating heart infarction patients to group-centred after-care (Rwd)
1.6	-	Group-centred after-care for women after mastectomy
2.1	Preparation for parenthood Physical exercise during pregnancy	-
2.2	-	Guidance of parents and child during a child's stay in hospital; the experience of a chronic disease and the PAGO-project
2.4		Exercises for correct lifting of heavy burdens
2.5	Self-activity training for elderly Groups for women during menopause	Preparation for retirement
4.1	-	Self-help within the patient organisation for Crohn's disease
4.3	Guidance by & for patients with multiple sclerosis	-

An enumeration of the appearance of self-activity of patients as a theme in the curriculum is presented in Table 5.

Table 5:   Survey of the (F), (C) and (S) places

Year	Form (F)	Content (C)	Suggestions for supplements (S)
1	2	0	6
2	4	3	4
3	4	0	0
4	8	1	1

In the fourth year the accent lies on formal presentations dealing with self-care. During this year the students work intensively on the 'problem-oriented record as a basic tool' (Weed, 1971), and much attention is devoted to self-care and the corresponding role of physicians. A good example is the input to block 4.3, where students and co-helpers meet and discuss the guidance by and for patients with multiple sclerosis. One of the features of the educational system at Limburg is that during a block students first formulate their own specific study goals; self-programming and problem solving are central educational goals. Hence the extent to which the self-activity of patients and the corresponding role of physicians is studied does not depend entirely on the form or content of the block books.

Self-activity of the patient can be considered as one of the 'red threads' which can be picked up in many aspects of the study material and then can be pursued by collecting information by research and by training. But before the specific thread can be found, together with many others, some basic introduction to the theme plays a facilitating role. Tables 3 and 4 show the blocks of the curriculum where explicitly or implicitly this red thread is already interwoven. It is realistic to assume that it can more easily be picked up by those students who are already sensitised to the subject through an option training or a student assistantship in the PAGO project. Our experience suggests that these students fulfil a role as co-pioneers in the educational system. They are the ones best able to influence fellow students from their group in studying the opportunities for self-activity on the part of patients.

The search for strategies to change conventional authority/dependency relationships remains tough and challenging. On the basis of carefully executed, but still far too few investigations, new lines of development can be drawn gradually, leading to more insights into the possibilities and limitations of self-activity with regard to one's own body. In this way one can reach towards a balanced dialogue between the two complementary kinds of expertise: the experiential one of the patient with his or her peers, and the medical expertise of the physician.

References

Bremer Schulte, M.,Cormane, R., Dijk, E. van & Wuite, J. (1982) 'Groepsbehandeling psoriasispatienten volgens de duo-formule (Group treatment of psoriasis patients according to the duo-formula), Nederlands Tijdschrift voor Geneeskunde.

Brouwer, W. (1980)'Arts en patient op hetzelfde spoor?' (Doctor and patient on the same track?) in M. Bremer Schulte, (ed.), Samen beter worden: nieuwe samenwerkingsvormen tussen patient en hulpverlener (Healing together: innovative co-operation between doctor and patient), Alphen a/d Rijn, Samson.

Council of Europe'Final report on the patient as an active participant in his own treatment', CDSP, 31, Strassbourg.

Levin, L., et al(1975) Self-care: lay initiatives in health, Prodist, New York.

Strauss, A.(1975) Chronic illness and the quality of life, Mosby Co., St. Louis,

Weed, L.(1971) Medical Records, Medical Education and Patient Care; the problem oriented record as a tool, Yearbook Medical Publishers Inc., Chicago.

HEALTH EDUCATION AND SELF-CARE IN LAPLAND
Bo Henricson

I am the district doctor in Arjeplog, Lapland, Sweden. I got my medical education in Denmark and Sweden and since 1975 have been employed as the district doctor at the local hospital in Arjeplog. I and two other doctors have complete responsibility for public health and medical care within the municipal district. This district consists of both high and low mountainous areas with a main highway passing through the town. The size of the area is 16,000 square kilometres and it has a population of 4,000. We have snow from mid-October to the beginning of May, which often causes difficult transport problems.

The local hospital where I work has, at present, 27 beds of which 21 are long-term medical patients and six acute. The standard is average for Swedish medical care, i.e. technically rather high. We have hardy people who do not come unnecessarily to hospital. As it can sometimes be difficult to get to a doctor many people practise self-care. Nevertheless, there seems to be a trend towards handing over more and more problems to established medical care. This is especially the case with those living close, i.e. in the town of Arjeplog, with its eighteen hundred inhabitants.

I have often received questions from patients showing that knowledge of even the most common illnesses is quite limited among the general public. It is not difficult to explain to the patient the causes and circumstances of his illness and this at a later stage contributes to a better understanding. During many public lectures on food, exercise and health, the curiosity of the participants has often been directed towards the causes and circumstances of an illness rather than focussing on the theme of the evening.

Because of the interest shown, the doctors discussed the benefits of holding public lectures about individual illnesses, their prevention and treatment. In 1977, working together with an adult educational institution in Arjeplog, we began lecturing about illnesses. That autumn we held ten lectures covering the most usual illnesses encountered in the daily work in our consultation rooms. We spoke in simple terms, handed out pamphlets and photostat copies in order to give the participants a better understanding. We even tried to initiate two-way communication with the participants which proved to be more successful than expected. We lectured for one hour after which we had half an hour for questions, discussion and group-work. The subjects were very commonplace, for example, sick children, heart attack, ulcer, backache, home medicines, etc. We advertised in local shops and in the waiting room at the hospital. We told patients which evening their particular illness was to be discussed and it often happened that people presented their own case during lectures. In that way we had free demonstrations which were appreciated by all.

There were 60 per cent women and 40 per cent men of ages ranging from ten to eighty years. It was a great success and we had an average of ninety people each evening, i.e. five per cent of the local population. Even the local press covered the activities.

We continued during the autumn of 1978-9 with chosen subjects and found that by the autumn of 1979 we had covered almost everything. So in 1980 we did not hold any lectures. Next we hope to start at the beginning again. When the majority of the people in the town had had the possibility of hearing us, we travelled to the various villages in the area and had almost 100 per cent support from the people.

As a result of this success, the adult educational institution in the north of Sweden employed me to teach leaders of self-care groups in the region. According to unofficial reports, the success was great and there have been many evening courses in self-care, from Kiruna in the North to Umea in the South. Together with a colleague, I have made shorter tours where we lectured on self-care and its possibilities to the Diabetic Association, the District Nursing Association, the Social-Medical Institutions in Umea and Uppsala, and to the general public in different large cities. I have experimented with non-smoking groups and anti-smoking campaigns but with doubtful results.

In the spring of 1981 I began lecturing in the school of Arjeplog and used the book 'Take Care of Yourself' by Vickery and Fries. I teach the 16 year olds and interest is high. I also have plans to teach in the lower classes (children between seven and ten years), and this will probably begin next year.

In Sweden we have a radio station which broadcasts basically music, news, plus two minute interludes of consumer information. I have contacted the radio station here in the North that reaches 250,000 people and have suggested that we could do a programme about self-care in the same way. This would reach the people who do not come to the lectures. The work involved would not be very great, as I intend to write to all my colleagues in the North and get them to write one or two self-care summaries concerning their work and field. These could then be sorted out and read into a tape-recorder, ready for use during the programme. I have already written a health-care summary and hope soon to receive a reply from the radio as to when we can start.

What are the reactions to our self-care measures? If one begins at the grassroots level, the reaction has been extremely positive. Between 3,000 and 4,000 people have attended our lectures, not to mention the self-care groups that have been working throughout the North. In the town of Arjeplog a so-called sports group was formed by older people. This was based on coming to our lectures, going on walks, eating correct food and other health care measures and has had spontaneous positive results.

If one goes one step higher, to the municipality, there has not been so much interest. We have offered to lecture on the physiology of ageing to politicians concerned with social welfare, but there has been no response to our offer. The school board is the only group that has shown interest by allowing us one hour per week at the school.

The county council, which is my employer, has on the whole been neutral. They no doubt want to see how things develop before they give their support. Unfortunately, one feels that they are more interested in medical care than in prevention, but as a result of the bad state of the economy this tendency may now change. I have experienced a positive interest among younger colleagues at medical school as well as in the hospitals and clinics throughout the country where I have lectured. Most complaints are related to the lack of manuals for self-care and patient education. I hope that through my own lectures I have given them enough support to get them started.

On the other hand older colleagues have reacted negatively, saying, for example, that it can cause extra work at the hospital. An older colleague said: 'When I held a lecture on breast cancer, I received many over-excited women in the consulting room and thus extra work'. The traditional role of the doctor still exists in Sweden and is difficult to change.

Here in Arjeplog we have a 'self-care' group that has no connection with the established medical care. It concerns the 'hottest' subject here now, to stop Pleutajokk. This group, 'Arjeplog People against Pleutajokk' is fighting to stop the municipality and a Swedish mining company from opening Sweden's first uranium mine in Pleutajokk in Arjeplog. The struggle is intensive and the outcome yet unknown. We also have a group that is fighting the chemical spraying of forests.

What have we gained from our lecturing? Many of our patients come to us with a diagnosis already in the back of their minds. They try to treat themselves before they come, sometimes with good results. They come for guidance or to confirm their own diagnosis, to be reported sick or to receive medical prescriptions.

Benefits are also gained via the telephone consultations which we have each morning. People often only need telephone consultations and guidance in order to take care of themselves at home. People have learned that the doctor is not an authoritarian figure trying to hide his professional secrets, but someone who tries to share his medical knowledge with them. This takes away much of the mystique surrounding the medical profession. Patients feel greater security in knowing that both doctor and patient are working towards the same end. We feel a greater sense of co-operation with patients and know that prescriptions are followed better when the patient understands the causes and circumstances involved. Unnecessary consultations have diminished in number because many illnesses are treated at home. People learn to know the workings of the local hospital and this saves much time.

I think that our work with self-care has given people a better quality of life as they lose some of the insecurity that exists in the stressful times of today. One learns to handle problems that influence one's health in such a way that one avoids ill-health without expecting others to become involved.

As can be seen from the above, we are average doctors with a normal work-load. We have no special qualifications to help us but we think that we have succeeded well with self-care. We recommend that others in established medical care follow our example. It may not be easy for the individual doctor but, at grass roots level, there is the possibility of influencing unfavourable developments in society in a completely new way.

As a final comment I can say that for the past five years the population in Arjeplog has not changed, but visits to the local hospital have decreased by nearly 20 per cent. I do not know whether this is a result of increased self-care, greater security in having permanent doctors, better health among the people, or our campaign to encourage people to try and help themselves before they come here. I see this decrease in hospital visits as one of the positive factors in our work.

RESEARCHING SELF-HELP: A SOCIAL SCIENTIST'S PERSPECTIVE
Jan Branckaerts

The aim of this paper is to dispel, if possible, certain misconceptions which have emerged in recent discussions of research on self-help as to how social scientists should study self-help groups. The ideas will be illustrated from experiences in studying self-help groups in Flanders (Belgium).

A principal misconception is the idea that self-help groups present a special case to social scientific study, and that this requires a particular kind of involvement in the observations made about the phenomenon. This is, in a sense, saying that the nature of the phenomenon determines its method of study. It can be argued, on the other hand, that the aim of the research into self-help determines the method of study, and that the aim is constrained, not by the phenomenon being studied, but by the resources available to the researcher and by the goals of those sponsoring the research.

This situation is, of course, not unique to self-help research; but investigators into self-help, perhaps because of the newness of their field, sometimes seem to neglect to take this pragmatic observation into account. Perhaps they do so in order to advance their particular methodologies for which they have previously been unable to gain acceptance; on the other hand, if their field of research does signal a genuine reorientation of social studies toward other than professionally organised phenomena, they may be struggling with the necessity of having to develop a genuinely new conceptual framework.

There seems to be a widespread belief that social scientists are presented with special challenges in the study of self-help because of the 'voluntary and autonomous' nature of the groups. Against this it can be argued that neither of these characteristics of self-help groups is unique, nor do they pose particular challenges to study.

Voluntary organisations are nothing new in society. The Church, for example, is a well established voluntary institution, and the functioning of church-related groups has long been studied by social researchers. Where self-help groups may present a special case is that many of them are in the process of organizing themselves or have only recently been formed.

The participants in such groups may, therefore, lack definite ideas about the group's particular identity, methods of operation and structure; in addition, there is still little data available for making comparisons among the newly formed groups. Some groups, such as those for the blind and the deaf, have been long-established, but have only recently labelled themselves as 'self-help'; hence the data and the concepts used in studying these older groups often do not lend themselves to a comparative study of self-help.

So-called 'autonomous' groups are also well-established in society. The family is a ready example of a group often termed 'autonomous', yet it is intimately linked to participation in society through friends, work, and dependence on social goods and services. In the same way, self-help groups function in connection with their families, hospitals and external resources; in this sense, they can hardly be said to be 'autonomous'. Indeed, one might question whether the groups' avowed quality of being autonomous is a useful concept to apply in studying them.

There also appears to be a belief that self-help groups are studied, at least partially, in order to understand and foster their development. This attitude puts the social scientist in the position of promoting self-help groups, as opposed to his usual role of simply investigating social phenomena and communicating the results of his research to others. Impartial research into self-help would probably demand that the researcher did not conceive of the existence of self-help groups as being necessarily beneficial. Groups might be suspicious of one claiming to do 'impartial' research, thinking that research not explicitly aimed at supporting 'self-help' might endanger their existence or damage their cause; but it is most often from a 'neutral' position that the researcher convinces the group members of the worth and importance of his research. In addition, a description of observations in neutral terms may open new perspectives, with potential gains for all concerned; it offers the possibility of discussing differing views of reality on an allegedly detached basis, and not according to the peculiarities of the worldviews involved. In any case, combining the ideas of 'understanding' and 'fostering' seems to imply that there is a communality of goals in the scientific study of self-help and social policy attitudes towards it: such may not always be the case.

This brings us to a point about the methodological requirements for the study of self-help. It has been stated that, since self-help groups are formed for highly personal reasons, they must consequently be studied on a personal basis. Such an assertion draws on the Weberian distinction between 'verstehen' and 'erklaren', for it raises the question of the extent to which self-help observers should actually sympathise and participate in the phenomenon. Proponents of the 'verstehen' approach argue that the theoretical structuring of the research should be postponed until the subjects of research develop their own conceptual understanding of the phenomenon of being investigated; in addition, 'verstehen' adherents hold that meaningful data can be gathered only if the researcher accepts the research subjects' system of communication.   According to this theory, the subjects are considered to be uniquely capable of formulating and expressing their views of reality. No one will deny the usefulness of such an approach, but at the same time it is obvious that reality as experienced and expressed by the insider is not the only possible reality. By emphasising that the observer has to be sensitive to the perceptions of the group participants, for instance, one may be led to ignore the dynamics of the group as a whole. One may only be making clearer what is already generally known or taken for granted about the attitudes of the group's individual participants.

However, a more useful contribution to knowledge about the phenomenon might be gained by taking the point of view of an outside analyst. Indeed, one might perceive more by taking a point of view contrary to that expressed by individual group participants, or perhaps by challenging certain expressed points of view in order to clarify them. In effect, a fruitful study of self-help might result from a form of intrusion into the groups and their ideas, as opposed to sympathetic detachment. It has been suggested that self-help groups have a special quality which comes from the process of sharing that goes on within them. For this reason, participant observation and other approaches common to this kind of study might be required. But here again, this methodology would be used in any study aiming to discover groups' or organisations' informal processes. This does not make research on self-help different from all other kinds of research.

In other words, one might not understand self-help groups simply by observing what the participants think about themselves or think they want. One might instead place the groups within a context of principles of social structuring, which itself might be influencing the behaviour of the actors within the groups. If this is the aim of the research, one need not necessarily collaborate with self-help groups beyond trying to communicate clearly with them. Collaboration, especially if carried too far, might go back to the idea of fostering the groups' development, and constructive scientific inquiry may not wish to assume such a preconceived attitude.

This last statement may sound contrary to the earlier assertion that constraints on research into self-help are dictated partly by the objectives of those sponsoring the research, which may in fact be to promote the phenomenon. If such is the case, these objectives may indeed serve to bias the results of any research, and those sponsoring a project should be well aware of this possibility.

To illustrate the ideas just presented, it may be useful to describe briefly the experiences of the Sociological Research Institute of Leuven University in connection with its examination of two specific self-help groups and one government sponsored survey into policy alternatives towards self-help. In describing these experiences, particular reference will be made to the way the conceptual and methodological approach was determined by those sponsoring the research and by the resources available to the researchers. In each case, there is an attempt to answer the following questions: Who requested or commissioned the research? Who paid for the research? What was the sponsor's objective in requesting or funding the research? How and why were these objectives modified by those carrying out the research? What were the methods subsequently chosen by the researchers in carrying out their research? What are the preliminary results of the research and the implications which might be drawn from them?

The first case involves families of psychiatric patients who have organised themselves into a national federation known as 'Similes'. Under a programme of government funding the federation contracted for research into the rights of psychiatric patients. Then, at the suggestion of the director of one of the psychiatric institutes with which it was associated, contracted for additional research into how the concept of 'self-help' might be related to the organisation. Two independent researchers were engaged on the project and at the end of six months were asked to co-ordinate their efforts with projects concurrently being undertaken into self-help by the Sociological Research Institute of Leuven.

The researchers had previously occupied themselves simply with trying to determine the relationship between Similes and self-help. Now, with the guidance of the Institute, they began to clarify what the federation was trying to find out in requesting research into self-help. Neither the federation nor the director of the psychiatric institute originally proposing the research could give a clear answer to the question.

Similes indicated that it was unwilling to continue the research beyond an additional six months when it would have to assume responsibility for part of its funding. It suggested that it might be useful to determine the characteristics of relatives of psychiatric patients who had not yet joined local Similes groups. When asked, however, the federation could give no satisfactory answer as to the characteristics of current Similes members. The researchers thus recommended that the six months remaining be used to determine this.

At first, the organisation was reluctant to approve of an inquiry into what might have been considered confidential information concerning its membership. It eventually consented to the proposed approach, aware that it might lead to gains in the federation's effectiveness and a clearer sense of its purpose and identity. Accordingly, in the limited time left for the research, the researchers decided to conduct interviews with pre-selected members of one local Similes group to obtain certain factual information about each group member's activities, and the exact relationship to the psychiatric patient being served.

The informant members, all from a single local Similes group, were selected on the basis of preliminary interviews with certain persons from the federation's list of members, who gave the names of those in the local group who would be best placed to have the factual information desired concerning other members. The information sought included: the age, sex and occupation of each Similes member, his or her relation to the psychiatric patient, and attendance at specified Similes meetings; the nature of the activities engaged in by the local Similes group; and certain information about the psychiatric patients allegedly related to the Similes membership - such as how often they were visited and whether indeed they had families.

The conclusions which emerged from this approach are remarkable. First, it was discovered that half of the supposed relatives of psychiatric patients in the group were in fact not relatives but simply volunteers associating themselves with the group. Secondly, the activities of the group were found to revolve mainly around organising recreation for the patients, rather than discussing common problems encountered as relatives of psychiatric patients. Common problems were sometimes discussed, but this never occupied an important place in referring potential members to Similes groups, and so to be crucial to efforts of the organisation to expand its membership. In sum, both the researchers and those sponsoring the research helped shape the course of the inquiry, which resulted in some rather surprising results that could have been missed had the research been less 'obtrusive'.

Furthermore, a number of useful practical measures were instituted as a result of the research. First, the Similes federation urged other local Similes groups to consider adopting the methods employed in the research to identify more clearly the characteristics of their own membership. Secondly, the local Similes group on which the original research was conducted used the results to re-organise itself so as to serve better the needs of its members. Finally, the local group began a programme to promote its image among nurses and social workers in associated psychiatric hospitals.

The second case involves the Belgian branch of Huntington's League, an international organisation of self-help groups for sufferers from Huntington's Chorea and their families. It is discussed more fully in another contribution to this book. Huntington's Chorea is a hereditary disease that causes progressive deterioration of mind and body and eventually results in death. The Belgian group was established in 1975 by a group of physicians working in a psychiatric hospital specialising in the treatment of Huntington's Chorea.

The director of the hospital applied for state funds for research on the group from the viewpoint of self-help. His object was to try and obtain additional information which might be useful in helping to prevent the spread of the disease. Other members of the group supported the research, feeling that it might lead to the provision of additional physical facilities. The project was given the title 'Prevention of Huntington's Chorea: a project of a self-help group'.

Although the aim of the research was clearly known, and the approach clearly delineated, that is, to study the group as a self-help group, there was no clear idea as to how who the study would contribute to the objective of helping to prevent the spread of the disease. Influenced by its member physicians, the group came to the opinion that some case studies of the dangers and destructiveness of the illness might be useful in order to mobilise politicians to fund better and more specific services for sufferers of the disease.

To convince politicians of the need to promote such services and programmes, the group, guided by the self-help researchers, decided that a comprehensive survey was needed to show, as far as possible, the many social consequences of the disease. To this end, it was decided that a wider population of actual and potential sufferers from Huntington's Chorea should be interviewed than those in the group itself. So the family tree of the group's members were investigated to identify and locate additional potential victims of the disease. From the list of potential victims thus determined, two additional Huntington's Chorea self-help groups were formed.

This broader population was then interviewed to elicit information as to the psychological and social consequences of the disease, and as to how its proliferation might be better prevented. Sufferers from the disease were asked such questions as the disease's effect on marriage plans, family planning, and the person's acceptance at work and in other social situations. Of potential sufferers, such questions were raised as to whether one would inform one's children of the risk of the disease, or refuse to have children because of the possibility of their contracting the disease. In short, the interviews were highly structured in order to obtain specific information about the sufferers' attitudes toward, and experience of, the disease.

Research continues on this project, and it is too early to present even preliminary conclusions. The points to be made, however, are the same as those which were observed with the first project. The objectives of the research were developed and modified to a certain extent as a result of the collaboration of the researchers with the group being studied; and the researchers are obtaining certain specific information as a result of 'intrusive' interviewing, which raised questions that would probably not otherwise be discussed.

The third example concerns an ongoing inquiry into the concept of self-help by Leuven University's Institute of Sociological Research. Originally the project was conceived simply to provide information about self-help groups existing in Flanders, a list of which had been compiled by the Institute. In order to obtain government funding for the project, however, it was necessary to modify its aim to include gathering information which might be useful in developing government policy towards self-help.

Once funding had been obtained, questionnaires were sent out to the previously identified Flemish self-help groups, but there was a very low rate of response. Consequently, social organisations which might work with or organise self-help groups, such as social welfare agencies or community mental health centres, were contacted to determine the names of additional self-help groups. From the list thus obtained, nineteen self-help federations were selected for detailed interviews, which are currently being undertaken.

Federations of local self-help groups were chosen because they already have a well-defined structure, probably representative of a fairly wide range of local views toward self-help, and because they seemed to be the most useful focus for the limited research resources available. These federations are being questioned largely as to their structure and functions, aspects which seem to have the most direct use for potential government policy. The federations are being asked to identify the resources open to them, their principal activities, problems they encounter, and approaches and means they take to remedy them.

Again, the main point to be made in describing this research is that it has been modified to suit the needs of its sponsors and the resources available to those carrying it out. Further, specific rather than 'open-ended' information is being sought from the self-help organisations being interviewed.

In conclusion, it might be said that research into self-help in Flanders demonstrates that a structured, rather than a 'sympathetic' approach may produce the most useful results. The method pursued in the research may in any case be determined by considerations outside the control of the researcher - namely the desires of those sponsoring the research and the resources available to the researcher - and may be modified in the course of the research by dialogue with the self-help groups being studied.

PART III SELF-HELP IN PRACTICE

THE PATIENT'S POINT OF VIEW
Alec Dakin and Jennifer Milligan

Introduction
Patient participation is a new but growing development in primary health care We write as patients who have been involved with one group in Bristol, England since it started five years ago, and we hope in this account of our group, which is known as 'The Practice Association', to show the strengths and the limitations of what has been achieved.

The practice
The practice, based since March 1975 in a health centre, is in a predominantly middle-class inner city area where the houses are mainly large and Victorian, many of them converted into flats and bedsitters. There are a higher than average number of elderly patients and a fairly large number of children and young adults. There is mobility of between 15 and 20 per cent per annum, mainly among young adults.

There are four partners, all in their thirties and early forties: the three men are full time and the woman does full consulting hours only. No deputising service is used. The practice, which is long established, has grown rapidly in the last ten years from about 3,500 to 10,000 - mainly through the closing of single-handed practices in the area. When our Association started in 1974, the practice list was about eight thousand.

The Association
The idea for starting a patients' association came from Dr T. Paine (1974) who as a member of an Open University course on systems behaviour had been impressed by the stress laid on the importance of feedback. He wrote a letter for patients which was left at the surgery during a period of several months and about one thousand copies were taken and read in that time.

The result was a meeting in February 1974 which was attended by about 40 patients, followed by a further meeting in April 1974, open to all patients, at which the first committee was elected.

Membership and constitution
The Practice Association is open to all patients and staff in the practice. By 1977 it was felt that our brief early constitution needed to be replaced by a more detailed one. At the same time the committee discussed the possibility of a small annual membership fee. Some felt this would give a greater sense of

commitment, but most were against this, arguing that all patients should be free to take as great or as small a part as they wished without any formal membership requirement. So all members of the practice are entitled to come to the Annual General Meeting and vote for the chairman.

The committee consists of chairman, vice-chairman, secretary, treasurer and eight members. The chairman and vice-chairman can hold office for only two years. Two ordinary members who have served three years must resign each year, but can stand for re-election after a year's absence. Co-options can be made. The community care co-ordinator, a member of the suggestions and complaints group, and the publicity organiser are always on the committee, which meets monthly. We are fortunate in having a receptionist and a health visitor on our committee. By mutual agreement no doctor serves on it, though doctors are invited in turn to attend.

We have always wanted the staff to feel part of the Association, and the quarterly lunchtime meetings between the committee and the staff have helped considerably. There have also been talks at our evening meetings from the nursing team, and - while we had them - from the health centre social workers.

Aims

The aims of the Association are as follows:

1. To give patients a voice in the organisation of their care;
2. To allow the expression of dissatisfaction and resolve the problem if possible;
3. To provide education and discussion on topics of interest;
4. To give voluntary community care help.

Work of the Association

The association has been active in the pursuit of its aims:

Aim 1

Giving patients a voice in the organisation of their care has been done by various means: through a suggestions box at the reception counter; through a suggestions and complaints group; through quarterly lunchtime meetings of the committee, doctors, health care team, receptionists, and administrator; and through annual evening meetings when all the doctors have answered questions from patients (Weightman, 1977).

Suggestions from patients have resulted in such innovations as a letter-box at the health centre, a ramp for wheelchairs, and notices about the slow working of the lift and the need to report to reception on arrival. We have been consulted by our doctors about changes in surgery hours, and we have been able to get some improvement in the several months' waiting time for chiropody. After representations were made to the District Administrator an extra session at the health centre was arranged.

Aim 2

In order to allow any dissatisfaction to be expressed and resolved, at the beginning a liaison sub-committee was set up consisting of three members. This was later called the Suggestions and Complaints Group. All the doctors, health care team and receptionists accepted this aspect of the Association's work and it was clearly understood that it would not deal with any matters involving medical judgement. Notices were put up and a section included in our annual card asking patients if they had a complaint to telephone a member of the Suggestions and Complaints Group or the chairman, or to make use of the suggestions box.

There have been only about four or five complaints a year, and a questionnaire prepared by the group and completed by 363 patients in one week in March 1976 showed that the large majority of patients were satisfied with all aspects of their care at the health centre. Some anonymous complaints put in the suggestions box have been so lacking in detail that nothing could be done about them.

We find that some patients who ring, however annoyed or angry, do feel considerable anxiety about letting the doctor know about their feelings, however well justified they feel them to be. Such complaints have tended to centre on the doctor's manner, that he has behaved in a brusque, insensitive or peremptory way, so that the patient has felt unable to express his needs. Having a member of the association available to listen to such problems seems to relieve the patients' feelings and gives the doctors some feedback.

Recently a patient stated that she had not received adequate warning about the side-effects of a drug she was taking. As a result our doctors have produced a small leaflet to be given to patients receiving a drug which might affect their alertness and another leaflet about the correct taking of antibiotics.

As another method of dealing with criticisms we are hoping to adapt the 'Speakup' sheet used by another association. This allows the patient to remain anonymous but ensures that the complaint and the response to it are written down in some detail. The Association committee member acts as 'postman'.

Aim 3

In order to provide education and discussion on topics of interest, we have had about nine evening meetings each year. We try to keep a balance between specialist subjects (heart disease, arthritis, acupuncture, marriage counselling) and more general preventive medicine (eating and health problems of old age, knowing your pills and potions.) The attendance varies considerably from 25 to over 100. This year (1978/9) we are planning two self-help groups, one on stopping smoking and one on losing weight, and half a dozen talks on other topics. It will be interesting to see how effective a more extended approach is.

As a result of a talk on yoga, we have had weekly classes for members of our practice in a local hall for the past three years, and these have been much appreciated.

We have a monthly morning group for mothers of young children, and they have a programme of talks of particular relevance to their needs.

Aim 4

Voluntary community care help is achieved by means of a co-ordinator, who is always on our committee, who receives calls from a doctor or other member of staff when there is need for such help as fetching prescriptions, shopping, transport, baby- or granny-minding, doing some regular visiting to a housebound person or some practical job such as gardening. Balancing about 50 volunteers with demand is not always easy and at times we may have lost volunteers who did not feel sufficiently used, but perhaps typical of the general feeling of volunteers is the remark: 'I've been glad to show in a practical way my appreciation of the care and help I've received at the health centre.'

During the past three years a fortnightly - and now weekly - lunch club for about 30 elderly and often housebound patients has been very successful. We are fortunate in having the use of a room and kitchen at the local Friends' Meeting House for a small fee. The lunch club also has outings in the summer and theatre visits. We have set up a working party to look at provisions for the elderly in our area and to see where the gaps are and whether we can do any work to close them. About twice a year the co-ordinator sends a newsletter to all volunteers, and we are now developing this to cover most aspects of our work and it will be made available to patients at the health centre.

A welfare rights group has been meeting at the health centre one morning a week for the past year and a half, but there has been only a trickle of referrals. It appears that the need for this is not being perceived, is not great or is being met by other bodies.

We have compiled a list of patients belonging to various national associations concerned with aspects of health. These patients are willing, when asked by a doctor, to explain to another patient the information, advice, or support their particular association can give.

Publicity

Local

From the beginning, communication was seen as a major difficulty, particularly as the health centre is shared with another practice which does not have a patient participation group and all wall publicity has to be in the entrance lobby and not in the waiting room.

In July 1974 we sent a letter to all homes in the practice so that at least at the beginning all patients should know of our existence and aims. Subsequently we have had to rely on other, less demanding methods.

Cards setting out the year's meetings and the Association's main functions are available at the reception counter and have been in use for three years; they have proved a useful innovation. At the beginning of each year we have delivered over 1,000 cards to patients in selected groups or roads, and last year we printed 4,000 in all. Previously we had had to rely on slips of paper distributed about three times a year.

Publicising meetings outside the health centre has not proved easy because we are only one practice in a densely populated area served by many doctors.

National

There has been more widespread publicity in national papers and periodicals and on local radio (Lyall, 1977). Several community health councils in other parts of the country have written asking for information. One patient represents our interests on the lcoal community health council, and we have taken part in community health council conferences on health centres and on the future of the health services in our area.

Finance

Finances have not presented any big problems. In the first two years we held raffles at evening meetings, but this has not been necessary recently. Our main outlay is the printing of the cards. Coffee at our meetings gives a small profit. Patients needing transport quite often make a donation (we pay volunteers 5p a mile). The luncheon club makes a reasonable charge for soup, sandwiches and coffee to cover its expenses. With only one fundraising effort this year (a cake stall at a local fair), we have a healthy balance. Donations are sometimes received from patients, or their relatives, when they are especially grateful for help given by the staff.

Conclusion

We hope that this account gives some indication of what can be achieved by a group such as ours. During the last five years we have gradually discovered ways of co-operating with the primary health care team to - we hope - the mutual benefit of patients and staff.

References

Lyall, J. (1977) 'Patient power', General Practitioner, 18, May 13.
Paine, T.F. (1974) 'Patients Association in a general practice', Journal of the Royal College of General Practitioners, 24, 351.
Weightman, G. (1977)'Off the pedestal', New Society,70, Jan. 13.
This article first appeared in the Journal of the Royal College of General Practitioners (1980) Vol. 30.

HYPERTENSION CLUBS IN CROATIA
Arpad Barath

Foreword by S. Kulcar

Nowadays in a community of about two thousand five hundred people we can expect to find as many as up to five hundred hypertensives. Traditional individual therapy should then ensure at least twelve half-hour visits to a physician or three thousand hours of physician's time per annum. Clearly no one can afford to provide as many as two physicians for a single disease in a relatively small community. Simultaneously there is the expanding phenomenon of $3 \times \frac{1}{2}$ of chronic diseases: half of the diseased still undetected, half of those detected not wanting the treatment and only half the quarter treated anticipating the treatment or actually actively implementing it. Particularly worrying here is the growing extent of non-compliance.

It is these factors that force us to look for other forms of care which will ensure the continuous and regular taking of medicines to control blood pressure, and control of excessive body weight and smoking. Whereas once only every fifth hypertensive would survive five years and there was a continually rising number of complications and premature deaths, today, given the correct measures, we can reduce strokes by a third and myocardial infarctions by a quarter. This of course is <u>by using regular procedures</u>. If the sick group itself takes over a large part of what were previously exclusively medical tasks (from blood pressure measurements to self-documentation and self-evaluation), the possibilities and achievements then became clear.

These introductory remarks to Barath's text underline the necessity of a search for new approaches. Our hypertensives' clubs or communities where the patients work in conjunction with their health workers certainly justify our five year investment of trouble and effort, but even more so they justify the hopes and courage of those who have boldly stepped into public health endeavours in the field of hypertension.

Background
The three-decade long development of and experience with self-management in Yugoslavia has now reached the point when self-reliance and mutual aid have ceased to be a mere free-choice alternative: rather, all citizens have a constitutionally defined right and duty to take an active part in managing their affairs in communities where they work, or in communities where they live or in both. (Ivanisevic et al., 1979).

Self-management, as a historical process, means decentralising the loci of decision-making and state power in such a way as to ensure the aggregation and mutual adjustment of diverse social interests and resources down at the most basic units of social life (work organisations, local communities, etc.); and the reverse, to ensure an equal, democratic representation of pluralistic interests upwards in the system of socio-political management, from these basic social units all the way up to the Federal Assembly. The mechanism of this two-way, dialectic process is a specific delegation and assembly system which, at all levels of the country's geo-political organisation (communes, associations of communes, republics, etc.) integrates three basic structures of public life (cf. Furtak, 1979):
- work place
- socio-political oganisations, and
- local communities.

This process did not and could not ignore the system of health care and social welfare and other systems of human services. Health and social welfare are neither theoretically nor in most practical senses (e.g. economically) the responsibility of any central authority - be it a state, a governmental agency or any other professional or organisational elite. Rather, it is the joint responsibility of all the three basic structures of social life listed above to pull together their social power and resources for planning and delivering health and social care for their own populations. This is the larger social context to which the hypertension self-care groups belong and contribute.

The emergence of hypertension clubs in Croatia
The initial idea that later shaped the emergence of self-care groups of hypertensive patients goes back as far as of 1962, when a small group of general practitioners, on the initiative of Dr Z. Kulcar, an epidemiologist and student of Professor Andrija Stampar (1888-1958), the founding father of Yugoslav social medicine and Chairman of the First World Health Assembly, made attempts to introduce certain forms of group work with these patients in their outpatient settings. This initiative, however, did not last long or include many people because it lacked wider social recognition and support both from professionals and from the general public.

In the following fifteen years, important changes occurred both in the epidemiological profile of the population (with a rise in the number of hypertensives, among other chronic conditions), and in the socio-political and professional context of health care. All these changes have encouraged primary health care workers, especially general practitioners with a long tradition, a firm educational background and sensitivity to community health, to develop more intensive preventive activities and establish wider and more flexible ties with community resources. As a result, the 'dormant' idea of group work with hypertensives re-emerged, but this time in an entirely new form. In the middle of 1976, a group of some ten general practitioners, along with Professor Kulcar and the present author, took a decisive step to establish clubs for hypertensive patients who, until then had been treated in the traditional manner, that is individually and relying mostly on medications.

The core innovative idea lay in the decision to let a number of patients <u>themselves</u> organise their own group on an independent, self-management basis. At the heart of this proposition was the principle of not attaching these groups to any segment of the formal health system (such as health centres of GP offices) where they territorially 'belong' as 'consumers' of primary care services, but rather to attach them to socio-political and other organisations or the larger communities where they live (local communities) or work (work organisations).

At the same meeting, a preliminary action programme was agreed upon, whereby each participating physician, along with his or her team, would initiate a wider socio-political process in the local or labour community leading to the establishment of at least one self-care club of hypertensives. The members of the clubs were to be recruited, in principle, from the population of patients whom the physician actually served.

The initiative was shortly afterwards shared with small groups of hypertensive patients who, in turn have taken over the task of mobilising the necessary community resources and other parties involved in social management of the given locality or work organisation. The physicians' responsibility has remained primarily at the level of informing and advising some of the patients to join the programme. By the end of the same calendar year (1976), three hypertension clubs had been constituted and were fully functioning: one was in a work organisation of Zagreb ('Jadran' Metal Furniture Factory), with a tradition of patients' (hypertensives and diabetics) groups of a similar sort. It had in total 42 members. Two other entirely new clubs were formed on the territory of a Zagreb commune ('Tresnjevka'), recruiting 64 members in total from the residents of two local communities (i.e. neighbourhoods). Two years later, that is in 1978, there were sixteen registered clubs of hypertensives over the republic with a total membership of about three hundred; by 1981 their number has increased to twenty-five, with a membership of over one thousand (Kulcar et al., 1981).

Basic guidelines

There are a number of quite distinctive characteristics of the hypertension clubs of Croatia which make them, on the one hand, quite similar to each other both in organisational form and functioning and, on the other hand, unlike any other form of 'group work' dealing with hypertensives run on a professional basis (sometimes boosted with the label 'self-care'), or other self-care endeavours run in a club-like, community-based fashion but again under the strong supervision or even 'programming' of professionals (e.g. clubs for treating alcoholics, clubs for elderly citizens, etc.). These distinctive features were set down at the very beginning of the project, and are as follows:

Clubs of hypertensives, formally defined, are voluntary organisations of citizens with chronically elevated blood pressure. Their principal common goal, aimed at by a wide variety of means, is to create socially independent, self-managing mechanisms for planned, permanent self-care and health maintenance. These mechanisms may well be complementary to the existing increasingly overburdened 'official medical mechanisms', but they should open wide perspectives for creating qualitatively new activities and treatment programmes for the members which previously were not available under the auspices of the professional services.

The decision both to establish and join these clubs must come from the patients themselves. The only professional help coming from their first-contact health workers (doctors, nurses) or other persons is restricted to informing and advising patients to join these clubs, if and only if such endeavour seems beneficial both for the individual and for the group as a whole.

Organisationally, the club belongs to the socio-political organising structure of a local or labour community and has rights and obligations on an equal footing with other social organisations concerned with questions of local significance. According to generally acknowledged self-management principles and the regulations of the given community, the membership of the club elects its own management (chairman, secretary, representatives, etc.) and regulates its own affairs through a number of legal documents (constitution, self-management agreements with other organisations, etc.), as needed.

Intensive co-operation of health workers, either as associate or active members, as representatives, part-time lecturers, or in any other form, is highly desirable, but to be carried out in a strictly unobtrusive way.

The club is not a place for instituting professional treatment (therapy) of any kind, even if health workers (doctors, nurses) co-operating with the club are the very same persons who care for members of the club in the framework of the 'official' health care delivery system (e.g. at the nearby health centre). The club is primarily a place of hypertension-oriented, social learning with an emphasis on mutual teaching, exchange of opinions and advice, and social activities.

The club is expected to represent an important linkage for better co-operation between health workers at large and the general public. It should provide stimulus, on the one hand, for its members to share in the responsibility for individual and community health in their immediate environment (family, local or labour community) and, on the other hand, to challenge professional groups for more active community health programmes, even including active teaching-learning programmes for medical students in community health and group work, among other things.

Contents of club activities

There are twenty-five clubs in different parts of the republic (Zagreb, Osijek, Karlovac, Pazin, Split, etc.). Their active membership of over a thousand makes up nearly one per cent of the republic's population of medically diagnosed adult hypertensives. The membership varies between twenty and sixty per club, with a mean of forty members. In principle, when the membership exceeds forty to sixty, a new club is set up within the same organisational framework of the particular local community, but with its own management body and programme.

Disregarding specifics, one may discern three commonly present groups of club activities:
- Self and mutual monitoring of blood pressure, body weight, eating habits, physical exercise and other aspects of members' own functioning, on a regular basis (at least once every two weeks);
- learning and pursuing specific behaviour programmes focusing on the control of various risk factors associated theoretically with high blood pressures;
- social activities and community action programmes, including activities initiated by the membership (e.g. home visits to absent members) or by other health related organisations concerned with the same community (e.g. the Red Cross).

The bulk of these activities are performed at club meetings, held every one or two weeks. The typical course of these meetings may be pictured from the following details.

The meeting starts with the checking over of the list of members for absentees in order to set up home-visiting groups for those who may need social help of any kind. Then a strictly observed blood pressure, body weight and/or other sign and sympton checking procedure follows. This is done in such a way that everybody may learn about everybody else's actual condition, and be able to make comparisons with figures from the last meeting as recorded in a club log-book. The same figures are registered in members' individual log-books too. This checking routine, needless to emphasise, gives plenty of opportunity for informal social interaction among members and with co-operating health workers (e.g. a nurse), if any are present, along with joking aroused by such 'funny' measurements as the belly circumference, which was introduced by one of the clubs. After this checking procedure, a formal lecture on a given topic may follow, given either by an invited professional (e.g. a medical doctor or a nurse) or by a lay-person, frequently a club member, who reports a specific experience worthy of common attention and group discussion. In many clubs, these formal lectures are usually accompanied or followed by other communication media, such as film presentations, group discussions with invited visitors, etc. Some clubs occasionally organise for their membership specific training courses held for all or for smaller groups of interested participants, such as courses in progressive relaxation, problem-solving techniques, or other behaviour modification techniques appropriate for individual or group practice. The two-hour long club meetings usually end up with reviewing forthcoming programmes and activities, and finally with informal chatting and small talk over a cup of tea and cake.

Club programmes, apart from regular meetings, also entail significant social events and ceremonies boosting the identity of the membership as a group. One of the most significant social events is the club's anniversary to which, apart from the active membership, acknowledged supporters and sympathisers from very different backgrounds (local authorities, representatives of various socio-political organisations, university people, medical students, representatives of other self-care clubs, etc.) are usually invited. At these occasions, persons with long membership are usually rewarded with diplomas and with some symbolic gift, and newcomers to the club receive their membership cards or other identity symbols (Matesa, 1981).

Leadership

The club is co-ordinated both in activities and in organisational matters by a representative body elected usually for a year from and by the active membership. This body usually includes the chairman, a secretary and a number of other persons for diverse tasks. All members have an equal chance to be elected for any of these functions, but once the representatives are elected, they receive special instructions from the former representatives, as well as instructions from the club's co-operating health workers concerning matters of group work, techniques for recording data etc.

Composition of membership

Regarding age, membership across the twenty-five clubs presently functioning in the republic shows considerable variation: one may find clubs that recruit mainly younger people, men aged up to forty, as well as clubs composed mainly of elderly people over sixty. Great variation in age within clubs is rare. This is because members' self- and mutual selection, mostly on the basis of personal knowledge and contacts, tends to bring together specific age groups. In contrast, most clubs recruit members with very heterogeneous professional and occupational backgrounds; it is not uncommon to see hypertensive housewives or semi-skilled industrial workers exchanging their thoughts, judgements or self-care advice and experience with lawyers, engineers or even with full-member hypertensive doctors or nurses.

One important characteristic that ought to be pointed out here is the requirement for strict homogeneity of the membership regarding two things: first, that all members are chronic hypertensives, and willing to focus their attention and interactions with other members, as far as joint club activities are concerned, solely and exclusively on that particular condition; and second, that none of the members suffer from any excessive behavioural or mental disorder that may interfere with groupwork. These two are the only recruitment criteria strongly emphasised in the entire system of hypertension clubs, as they are conceived and expected to offer reasonable help to those suffering from hypertension.

Resources and facilities

Both the financial resources and other facilities (e.g. meeting rooms, technical equipment, communication facilities) are provided by the local or labour community where the club organisationally belongs. Direct financing by members of their own club activities or of parts of them is left to their own decision. This usually amounts to a symbolic, rather low membership fee, voluntary donations for purchasing some items of technical equipment for common or individual use (such as blood pressure meters) or support for social events or activities. Many clubs, apart from the resources reserved for them in wider community budgets, occasionally receive donations from outside the local or labour community (such as from the Red Cross, a health centre or factory, etc.).

Role of professionals

As the reader may have inferred already, the role of professionals in the case of hypertension clubs is well-balanced and realistic, unlike the situation in the self-care movements of many other (mostly developed) countries. This is not to say that from time to time, in some places, discussions do not become overheated. Of course, they do. But these almost exclusively represent controversies among professionals themselves, and they are practically absent from dialogues between professionals and the general lay public.

In brief, some professionals are permanently involved with the issue of self-care, either theoretically in line with the general trend in the republic's public health, or quite practically by having responsibilities in helping and co-operating with one or another self-care club and its recruitment of patients. However, such active professionals concerned with self-care make up only a small number of all professionals engaged in health matters. The majority of the health labour community (e.g. nurses, health workers, psychologists, sociologists, social workers etc.) do not take any particular role in self-care endeavours. This is because either they are simply not aware of the potential of self-care and community programmes in contemporary health (except for some generalities gleaned from the mass media), or they simply ignore the whole issue, never having been 'forced' to learn or to do anything for their patients' socially organised self-care. Many of them reason that self-care falls outside the scope of their everyday professional practice.

As far as the functioning of hypertension clubs is concerned, their organisational independence (i.e. located outside the formal structure of the health care delivery system), makes them a kind of ideal co-operative composed and governed by the patients themselves and some of their professional helpers, mainly primary health care workers. The role and actual contribution of these active professionals certainly varies, depending on their professional, personal and/or socio-political expectations. At some places one may see and meet, for instance nurses who speak and act rather over-protectively in the name of 'their' clubs using such terms as 'our family'; alternatively, it is also possible to meet general practitioners who, beyond occasionally attending club meetings or advising their patients to join the club, know little about what patients are up to once they become active in the club. Beyond these variations, however, there is a trend towards increasing independence on the part of hypertension clubs from their co-operating professionals. The relationship of the two parties, at the very beginning, usually starts with much emotional attachment on both sides, while later it develops into a realistic partnership in which they appear on an equal footing in terms of knowledge, attitudes and skills concerning hypertension. Many 'old timer' club members happen to know and can better explain to their peers things concerning self-care skills than can doctors or nurses. They rightly receive the joking nickname of 'professors'.

This is by any reckoning a healthy trend towards maturation of the self-care and mutual aid endeavours, telling more about their progress than would any evaluation data or statistics. This maturation process, we may add, is best observed in clubs where there is continuous collaboration between the two parties, and the chairperson has a decisive role.

Some evidence of outcome

Even if available, it would be very hard to say what evaluation data should or could be used for making judgements concerning the outcomes of the clubs' endeavours. Comprehensive 'in-depth' research on self-care processes and the outcomes that may follow from the diversity of club activities and related life-events has not been carried out. There would be a great number of methodological obstacles (lack of comparable control groups, obtrusiveness of detailed research protocols, unequal communication skills and literacy among various segments of club members, etc.) to be faced. Until now the five-year development of and experience with self-care hypertension clubs has not encouraged us to undertake excessive inquiries into the potential long-term effects, such as on mortality and morbidity rates, resistance to stress, mental health functioning, and the like. But possibilities for such investigations are now, as of 1981, opening up.

What we can offer at this moment are some general findings gathered by way of exploratory studies, subjective reporting of club members, and the like. We may summarise them as follows.

One of our early pilot studies (Barath, 1977; Kulcar et at. 1978) done in two clubs with a total of some forty members, suggests that the mean rate of blood pressure in this particular group of subjects significantly decreased in the course of the two years of club activity that were observed; that is, for the great majority of particpants blood pressure was contained within the limits of clinically non-alarming variation. This result, however, was found to interact statistically with the age of the subjects.

In the same study, efforts were made to get some insight into some aspects of mental health/general health funcioning of the examined subjects, as these might have changed in the course of their club membership over the initial period of two years. A shortened and adapted version of Goldberg's (1972) General Health Questionnaire was administered in interview form and a significant increase was noticed in mean scores, suggesting better mental/general health functioning. The most striking differences related to sleeping habits, and the quality of resting time, greater enjoyment of social activities and of every-day work, and less depressive thoughts, among other things.

Many observers report a significant increase/strengthening of group cohesiveness among club members. One of the most commonly reported indicators of this is the fact that 'old' members, i.e. those who have completed their self-care programme and have controlled all clinical signs and symptons for their formerly 'bad' cardio-vascular functioning, do not stop attending club meetings, nor do they change habits recently acquired from the recommended self-treatment programme. Instead, they keep coming to club meetings and maintaining their life 'regime' like any other well-motivated 'newcomer' to the club.

The presentation of certain behaviour modification techniques, such as progressive relaxation, to a restricted number of club members aroused great interest not only among those who actually took part in these sessions, but also among a huge number who had never had the chance to attend these meetings. So many clubs have expressed the aim of making these or similar behaviour modification techniques and related technologies (such as tape recorded instruction packages) more readily accessible for wider use.

Initial observations have been started (Grahovac, 1981) concerning the life expectancy of club members. Initial data suggest that among club members one may find significantly lower rates of fatal attacks, along with a relatively low rate of myocardial infarctions and strokes, as compared with the general population of patients suffering from the same chronic condition.

Further research is required from the entire population of present and future club members. This means a long-term investment is needed on the part of the entire scientific community of the republic's health care system, along with understanding and help from society as a whole to cope with this 'silent killer' called hypertension.

References
Barath, A. (1977) 'Evaluacija jednogodisnjeg rada klubova hipertonicara' 76-77 ('Evaluation of one year's experiecne with clubs of hypertensives' 76-77), working paper, mimeo, Zagreb.
Furtak, R.K. (1979)'Yugoslavia: A Speical Case', in Hayward, J.E.S. and Berki, R.M. (eds.) State and Society in Contemporary Europe, Martin Robertson, London.
Goldberg, D.P. (1972) The Detection of Psychiatric Illness by Questionnaire, Oxford University Press, London.
Grahovac, V. (1981) 'Osnivanje i nacin rada klubova kronicnih bolesnika'. ('Organisation and work in clubs of chronically disabled'), paper presented to the workship 'Uses of self-help in health care for hypertensives', mimeo, Zagreb.
Ivanisevic, S., Pavic, Z. and Ramljak, M. (1979) Samoupravljanje, (Self-management), Skolska Knjiga, Zabreb.
Kulcar, Z. et al. (1978) 'Controlling hypertension: community care and mutual aid through neighbourhood clubs', WHO Chronicle, 32,448-450.

Kulcar, Z. et al. (1981) 'Mjesna zajednica i program mjera zdravstvene zastite u SRH za razdoblje 1981-1985', (Local communities and measures of health care in SR Croatia for the period 1981-85), working paper, mimeo, Zagreb.

Matesa, S. (1981) 'Program edukacije bolesnika, osnovne teme programa', ('Patient education: basic course programmes'), paper presented to the workship, 'Uses of self-help in health care for hypertensives', 12 December, mimeo, Zagreb.

HEALTH CLUB NETWORK DEVELOPMENT IN SOUTH HUNGARY
L. Szilard, A. Ozsvath and J. Tenyi.

Introduction
The majority of people suffering from cardiovascular diseases are unknown to their GPs (Reid, 1974). And the choice of consulting a doctor was found to be tenth in order of rank when people had health problems (Freer, 1980) and, according to Bradshaw's estimate, about 80-85 per cent of all the diseases and health problems are treated without any consultation with a doctor (Bradshaw, 1977). The attitude of medically cared for patients is also far from ideal. In West Germany, for example, nearly half of the hypertensive patients fail to take their medicines regularly (Reithling, 1980).

According to Pflanz (1982), in the relationship between health services and the community the following problems can arise:
(a)   Fear of: highly technicised, dehumanised medicine; serious diagnoses; discovery of latent diseases; mistakes in doctors' jugement; and consequences of the diagnosis in private life.
(b)   Difficulties in communication because of: shortage of time; medical jargon; and emotionless rationality.
This points to an increase in self-help and self-care.

On the 1st January 1982, within a WHO framework a 'Comprehensive Cardiovascular Community Control and Monitoring Programme' (Tetra CP) was started in the town of Pecs and a part of county Baranya (South Hungary). Tetra CP consists of three main components:
1. the follow-up of the morbidity and mortality trends;
2. the follow-up of the change (if any) in the frequency of major risk factors by representative medical screening and
3. health educational intervention.
The health educational intervention is planned to be introduced at two levels:
1. health education of the whole population of the project area;
2. health education directed at the high risk population discovered by screening.
The expectations of group-directed health education are high. It is well known from Levin's (1943) research that discussions and group activities are more effective in bringing about changes in life-style than any other strategy. This theory makes an obvious case for basing our 'high risk population directed' health

educational plans on group dynamics, ie. on the club form. But club life has no real tradition in Hungarian society and community initiatives are very rare, as is the spontaneous formation of any kind of club. In the field of health, most of the few clubs are connected with mental health problems and alcoholism (e.g. clubs of former alcoholics etc) (Fekete, 1980; Gerevich, 1979; Sule, 1975).

The formation of all these clubs was inspired by the national health service system. In our opinion, in the field of preventive care of those at risk, the most feasible way would be to establish health clubs based on the catchments/geographical boundaries of the existing health service system, namely on the basis of the GPs' network. This suggestion seems reasonable because GPs' opinions are, even today, highly esteemed, especially among rural populations. This form of health education also accords with international efforts as well (Selecta, 47, 1981; Troschke, 1981).

In order to gain more experience with risk group directed health education, and to check the acceptability of the programme to the Hungarian rural population, we organised a pilot study connected with cardiovascular screening.

The whole adult population of the Hungarian village of Nagyharsany was screened with a non-invasive cardiovascular screening method (Szilard, 1979; Szilard, forthcoming). Patients found to be ill or with a high risk of cardiovascular diseases were summoned for further medical investigation. Ten to fifteen patients with a similar condition, ie. cardiovascular disease, were asked to attend the local health centre regularly. While they were waiting to be seen a medical doctor, trained in group dynamics and health education, initiated a discussion about healthy ways of life, habits, personal health problems and of ways to solve them.

The results of the pilot study show that this kind of health education is acceptable to the Hungarian rural population. It was found that the rate of participation and the activity of the screened inhabitants were good; and that, the most suitable method of leading these groups is to start with a 'directive' approach, gradually moving to a semi-directive kind of leadership.

Based on the experiences mentioned above, our project team has constructed the first version of a plan for developing a health club network which incorporates the following considerations:
1. Health clubs must be closely connected with the locally based health service systems.
2. GPs and/or their staff should be trained to lead these groups.
3. The adult population of the project area should undergo regular multiphasic medical screening.
4. GPs should be informed by the screening centre of any high risk patients.

5. Such high risk patients should be summoned for medical consultation with their GP at the local health centre, not more than twenty at a time. At the health centre waiting room discussion about health problems must be initiated with a view to encouraging them to join the local health club.

6. In forming health clubs, local authorities and organs of public culture should provide significant help and cooperation to the project staff (e.g. in the placing, planning and organising of programmes etc).

7. Health clubs should provide two types of programmes:
   (a) small group sessions led by health professionals using a directive form of leadership. Topics to be discussed are risk behaviours, healthy ways of life, possibilities for changing habits and personal problems;
   (b) ordinary club programmes on health nutrition, ways to give up smoking, physical activity, sports and 'stress-free' living, etc.

8. A regular mental health service is also planned to be included in the health clubs.

9. At a later stage, leadership of the health clubs must take a non-directive form, helping members to rely on their own initiatives in running their clubs. In this way, health clubs would serve as centres of a self-care movement and at the same time form a bridge between the community and the health service system.

Medical screening will begin in March 1982; postgraduate courses for GPs and their medical staff are going to be organised in the second half of 1982 and, at the end of the year, we hope to establish the first health clubs.

References

Bradshaw, J.S(1977) 'British barefoot doctors?', Royal Society of Health, 97.

Editorial (1981) 'Gruppenarbeit durch den Allgemeinarzt: Problem-Patienten eine Brucke bauen', Selecta, 47, 3475-3477.

Fekete, J. (1980) 'Alkoholellenes klubok szerepe a rehabilitacionban', Alkohologia, 11, 159-161.

Freer, C.B.(1980) 'Self-care: A health diary study', Medical Care, 18, 853-861.

Gerevich, J. (1979) 'A Moravcsik Klub mukodese', Alkohologia, 10, 73-76.

Levin, K. (1943) 'Forces behind food habits and methods of change', Bulletin National Research Council, 108, 35-65.

Pflanz, M. (1969) 'Medizinsoziologie', in Hdb. der empirischen Sozialforschung Bd.2 Enke, pp.1123-1156, Stuttgart.

Reid, D.D. et al. (1974) 'Cardiorespiratory diseases and diabetes among middle-aged male civil servants', The Lancet, 469-473.

Riethling, A.K. et al. (1980) 'Ergebnisse eines Befragung von Patienten einer Hypertonia - Sprechstunde in ihrem Einnahmeverhalten', Z. arztl. fortbild, 74, 23.

Sule, F. (1975) 'Alkohol betegek csoportpszichoterapias modszerenek vizsgalata', Alkohologia, 6, 168-174.

Szilard, I. et al,(1979) 'Szamitogepes kiertekelessel egybekotott keringesrendszeri kerdoives eloszures modelljenek kialakitasa I-II', Nepegeszsegugy, 60, 257-271.

Szilard, I. et al. (forthcoming) 'Possibility of recognising latent cardiovascular morbidity: a computer assisted non-invasive screening method', La Sante Publique.

Troschke, J.V. and Riemann, K. (1981) 'Gruppenveranstaltungen zur Patientenaufklarung durch den frei niedergelassenen Kassenarzt', Deutsches Arzteblatt, 47, 2248-2252.

SELF-HELP IN THE SOVIET UNION: THE CASE OF THE DEAF
Madeline Drake

Voluntary social service, or obshchestvennost, is cherished by Soviet constitutional theory. The withering away of the State, conceived as the ultimate goal of communism, will be achieved, it is thought, only if people take an active part in government, the economy, health and social welfare. This is how a handbook for Party Activities put it: "Building communism is the task of the whole people, of each Soviet citizen. On his awareness, initiative, cultural development and professional expertise depends the successful achievement of the communist economic programme."(1) This is the thinking which inspires the widespread use of self-help and voluntary work throughout all spheres of Soviet life. In many areas of work, particularly those to do with welfare and health, lay workers greatly outnumber paid officials.

There are two different ways in which non-state effort is harnessed in these spheres. The first is through individual voluntary workers. These are recruited by the Communist Party, the Komsomol and the trade unions, and are attached to paid local authority health or welfare workers, who train and manage them. Such voluntary workers operate within the State organs. The second way is through self-help (samoobsluzhivanie). This term applies to those independently set up bodies which are organised by and for specific client groups. In Spring 1979, as a member of a delegation from the British Department of Health and Social Security, I visited one such organisation. This was the All-Russian Society for the Deaf, a self-help organisation which dates from the pre-Revolutionary era. This body provides an interesting model of how a self-help organisation can exist without a dependence on direct State funding, whilst benefiting from indirect subsidies.

We met the President of the Society at one of its industrial training enterprises in Leningrad. The President, in common with many of its staff, was deaf. Our visit was attended by a deaf and dumb interpreter, since lip-reading is not common in the Soviet Union. The Society's aim was to offer cradle to grave care for the deaf. It provided eight special schools and two kindergartens for deaf children in Leningrad alone; and two of its seventy industrial enterprises were in Leningrad. The Society builds its own housing, schools and leisure centres, and it lobbies for the interests of the deaf in all spheres.

The industrial training enterprise we visited trained deaf workers in electrical engineering trades. The enterprises are not like the British occupational workshops for disabled groups. The Soviet training enterprise operates like a normal factory and prepares workers to enter the mainstream hearing work force if they so wish. It appears that deaf workers are in demand because they are conscientous and well trained. But the enterprise director, a hearing man, said the workers were not yet able to compete for top jobs because the training enterprises do not have a capacity in the prestigious electrical trades. He had just started a new apprenticeship scheme in this area of work. The working day at this factory is from 7.30 a.m. to 4.30 p.m. The plant seemed outdated but serviceable. Homework is organised for the housebound and this is paid on piece-rate. Workers enter from the Society's schools or from the mainstream work-force. They serve a two-year apprenticeship and may then stay or go on elsewhere. The director felt that there was a tension between the requirements of industrial competition and the requirement to carry out work suited to the deaf workers' needs and abilities. Thus he had recently rejected a proposal to introduce very detailed work, since this might strain the workers' eyesight. He said that eyesight was even more important to the deaf than to the non-deaf, and he could not risk his workers' eyesight, even though the work would have been profitable.

It is of particular interest to note how the Society organises its finances. Its activities are paid for from the profits of its enterprises. It has no central government funding. It has the right to spend its income as it wishes, subject to approval by the local authority social security department. The profits are used to pay the Society's staff, and to pay for the housing, leisure and schooling of deaf people. The local authority build the accommodation, but it is planned and paid for by the Society.

A deaf worker will live in an enterprise flat when he works at the factory and will be able to stay on when he goes to work elsewhere. Deaf workers, like all Soviet citizens, are entitled to municipal housing, but they prefer the Society's flats. Enterprises for the deaf provide a complex of housing and other services for workers; and indeed it is a frequent practice for ordinary factories to provide such facilities for their workers. This system comes as something of a surprise, at least to the British observer. It dates from before the Revolution, when welfare was largely enterprise-based. Now the State is the leading partner in welfare, housing, educational and medical provision, but the enterprise retains much of its importance in this field.

The All-Russian Society for the Deaf is entirely self-supporting. However it receives an indirect government subsidy. This takes the form of a preferential rate of tax on its enterprises' profits. Thus, even though the productivity of deaf workers is ten per cent lower than that of hearing workers, the lower rate of profit tax paid by the enterprises of the former means that they make higher profits than do mainstream enterprises. Because of this, deaf workers received high productivity bonuses.

Thus, this system benefits the individual workers both by allowing them to earn reasonable wages, and by enabling the Society to provide various services for their needs. The workers also benefit by receiving a disability pension from the local authority social security department. Such a pension is paid to all disabled people in proportion to their disability, and graduated according to earnings. Generally the amount earned by workers in these enterprises is equal to the average Soviet wage plus productivity bonuses. Those who are too disabled to work full-time or efficiently and who, therefore, earn a smaller wage, receive more by way of pension. Thus, the deaf enterprise receives in effect two forms of indirect subsidy: as well as the preferential tax rates from the Republic government, it receives disability pensions for its workers from the local authority. The latter ensures that less efficient workers' incomes are maintained at little cost to the enterprise.

There is little exchange of money between the State organs and the deaf enterprise, and little between the latter and other enterprises. The deaf enterprise makes components for other factories in return for materials and the training of its workers. So, the Soviet welfare system is able to avoid the situation often operating in Britain, whereby money paid out by one department is then clawed back by another department.

The All-Russian Society for the Deaf is very closely linked to the government, even if financially independent from it. It is important for the Society to have a voice at all levels of government so that it can lobby effectively for its interests. The Society is devolved through the same hierarchical levels as the government: the Republic, the Regional and the District levels. The Society's officials attend the monthly local authority executive committee meetings when matters relevant to its interests are discussed. Most day-to-day contact is with the local authority social security department. The local authority social security department helps the Society in negotiations with the housing and planning departments on its building programme.

An important part of the Society's work is to lobby for its interests and to influence public opinion so that there is more recognition of the needs of the deaf. It appears to be an effective lobbying organisation. The President told us with some satisfaction of how they had managed to reverse an originally negative local authority response to the Society's application to build a Palace of Culture - leisure centre - for the deaf in Leningrad. The Society lobbied local authority members and stimulated public discussion on the issue. As a result, the Palace of Culture was included in the city plan.

According to popular Western views of the Soviet Union, the State holds a monopoly over all aspects of the citizens' lives. However, in practice, this turns out not to be the case. The State enters into a partnership with voluntary organisations. It also incorporates volunteer workers into its own governmental structure. Voluntary organisations such as the one described above appear to have a wider range of activities than comparable British organisations, since, as we have seen, they offer proper employment, professional training, education, leisure and housing to clients. This is made possible by the fact that they are allowed to make profits to finance themselves. They receive no direct subsidies: the indirect subsidy to the Society's enterprises is delivered through the tax system as a preferential profits tax. Workers are also subsidised through the social security system. So these organisations do not have the problem of being dependent upon central or local government for grants in order to continue to exist; and an elaborate machinery of grant-giving and receiving which would otherwise be necessary for the running of such bodies, is thus avoided.

Reference
1. K 100-letiyu so dyna rozhdeniya Vladimira Ilicha Lenina. Tesisy Tsentral 'nogo Komiteta Kommunisticheskog partii Sovetskogo Soyuza. Sparochnik partiinogo rabotnika Vypnsk 10i,1970,p.59.

THE BELGIAN HUNTINGTON LEAGUE: A CASE STUDY OF THE COLLABORATION BETWEEN PROFESSIONALS AND LAY PEOPLE IN A SELF-HELP GROUP
Jan Branckaerts

The aim of this paper is to describe the Belgian Huntington League (HL). This self-help group is remarkable in that it established itself in a fairly short time and collaborates closely with professionals. The following topics will be dealt with: what is Huntington's Chorea?; history and activities of the group; the research project; actual functioning of HL; the relations with the professionals and the International Huntington Association (IHA).

What is Huntington's Chorea?
In 1872 George Huntington, in an article entitled 'On Chorea', appearing in the Medical and Surgical Reporter, described for the first time an hereditary chorea affecting a few families in New York. The features of the disease have been little added to since then. What is known about it now can be summarised as follows. It is an inherited brain disease which affects individuals of either sex, each of the children having a fifty/fifty chance of inheriting or escaping the defective gene. The symptoms usually begin to appear between the ages of twenty-five and forty, usually after the genes have already been passed on to a new generation. The disease often shows itself by jerking and twitching movements, abnormal gait and slurred speech. Sufferers often show mental deterioration and marked personality changes, often leading to insanity and suicide and invariably to a slowly progressing dementia, total incapacitation and death. As can be inferred from this rather cold description, Huntington's Chorea takes a terrible physical, emotional and financial toll on the afflicted and their families. Moreover, it is often difficult to diagnose and no cure or predictive test is available at present.

History of the group
The history of the Belgian Huntington League cannot be understood without tracing it back to the original American roots. The famous American folksinger Woody Guthrie suffered from Huntington's Chorea. After being hospitalised for a period, his devoted wife, Marjorie Guthrie, started to consider her husband not only as the victim of Huntington's Disease, but also as the victim

of ignorance and institutionalisation. She began to think about how she could help Woody but also about how to help others. She read whatever little scientific information she could find and, with the help of the Secretary of the Interior, she contacted the National Institute of Health.

Because of the lack of information and research, she stimulated the formation of a Research Group on Huntington's Chorea as a part of the World Federation of Neurology, and induced scientists to publish a bibliography on this disease. In so doing she established from the beginning a close link between herself and the scientists. However, Marjorie Guthrie also felt that she had to organise the families. After the publication of a first appeal in the newspapers, she was able to locate thirty-five Huntington families after one year and to publish a first newsletter. In this newsletter the organisation that labelled itself 'The Commitee to Combat Huntington's Disease (CCHD)', described its goals as: research, education and assistance. CCHD started to attend meetings of neurologists and to appear on local radio and television.

The growing identification of potential sufferers had at least two consequences. First, it became clear that Huntington's Chorea was not so rare a disease, so more research funds could be advocated. Second, local branches could be organised in different areas.

These local groups give people the opportunity to explore feelings, attitudes and needs. As Marjorie Guthrie says, 'We are developing a network of hope and it begins when people care and share'. This message of hope could not be restricted to the American continent and soon Marjorie Guthrie started to initiate groups in other countries. In 1974 Dr Franz Baro, Director of the University Psychiatric Hospital, who had already studied Huntington's Chorea, organised the first biennial meeting of the Research Group on Huntington's Chorea of the World Federation of Neurology in Leuven. On this occasion he created the opportunity for ten Belgian Huntington families to meet Majorie Guthrie. As a result of this meeting the families started a Belgian group.

For five years some fifteen to thirty people met monthly in one of the members homes. This group consisted of potential Huntington sufferers as well as volunteers. These volunteers included medical doctors, scientists and students who professionally or in their studies were involved with Huntington's Disease problems. Since the disease is severely handicapping, sufferers were unable to attend the meetings as they were often too weak to endure transportation or unable to speak. Most of the members were people at risk of contracting the disease.

During these gatherings, information was gathered on the disease and its consequences. This included not only medical information about symptoms and treatment, but also information on psychological changes in the patient, reactions of the family, economic consequences and aspects of hospitalisation. Obviously all this entailed a lot of emotions. As a consequence, the exchange of experiences and the common search for solutions created an atmosphere of support and assistance. The attendance of professionals and potential sufferers proved to be mutually beneficial: potential sufferers were eager to hear professional opinions, while at the same time professionals learnt how to deal with delicate matters, such as how to inform people unaware of the heredity and the devastating aspects of the disease.

These monthly meetings, 'discussion-meetings', were complemented by two other kinds of gathering. As new members arrived, it became clear that the same problems had to be dealt with again: this was the start of topical conferences on specific subjects, such as heredity, medical insurance, employment and others. A second kind of gathering was organised for specific groups such as partners of the already afflicted or the healthy partners of potential sufferers. Another subgroup concentrated on the young.

None of these groups turned out to be successful. Among other reasons this was due to the fact that too much negativism accumulated without the compensating wisdom and experience of adults and of potential sufferers who had hitherto escaped the disease or of families who had coped well with the problems. Also the fact that specific problems were not related to the broader context of the problem, nor balanced by the more 'objective' view of sympathetic volunteers did not help.

After five years, a particular event encouraged a reconsideration of the organisation and functioning of the group. During one 'living-room' meeting all the professionals and families were assembled and two new members wanted to join the group. Everyone felt that the 28 people present were too many for a discussion of personal problems in an intimate way.

It was then decided to evaluate the group's position. The result was the start of two groups each concentrating on distinct geographical areas, but meeting yearly at a joint social gathering. These groups ran in this way for a while, but it soon became clear that the cohesion between the members was such that they would try to attend all meetings, wherever they took place. So, it was decided to continue as one group.

Another result of the evaluation was the beginning of a one-day family visit to one member's farm for walking, talking and eating. This was the start of a tradition known as 'the farm day': a unique gathering of all those involved with Huntington, serving also as a celebration of the sharing and friendship that developed during group meetings and through the informal telephone networks.

As to finances, until then the only funds that the League had at its disposal consisted of an equivalent of a $10 membership fee per year, per family. For its paperwork and administration it depended largely on the secretarial facilities of the hospital where some of the professionals were working. More specific problems of members were referred to sympathetic specialist professionals who handled them for free.

The group felt a real need to share it's experiences with other, until then unreached, Huntington's Disease families. However, members, volunteers and friends could not cope with the many and diverse problems and requests any longer, so the League decided that a more global, continuous and structured approach was needed.

This structured approach was formulated in terms of employing professional workers like a social nurse and a social worker. A project was submitted to the Flemish Federal Secretary of State for Welfare. The project was promoted by two members of the League, a university professor and director of a hospital and a psychiatrist. This combination of roles provided the scientific guarantee requested by the government, since funding could only be obtained for 'research and development' and not for development of a group as such. Additional support in terms of charisma and internationally acknowledged moral leadership came from Marjorie Guthrie who was visiting Belgium at the time. When approaching the Minister for grant aid, she made it clear that it was the government that had a problem and that she was going to help them solve it. The solution - so it was stated - was self-help. The government accepted the remedy and granted the research project.

The research project

The research project was given the title 'Prevention of Huntington's Chorea: a project of a self-help group'. The aim of the research was to approach the multiple problems of the disease by means of self-help activities.

It was decided that this could be done by developing a comprehensive survey in order to show the consequences of the disease and, at the same time, using the interviews from the research as a way of contacting people and bringing them together to form new groups. Problems that came to light during the interview could be discussed during the group meetings. Thus the project combined information gathering, social work and propaganda for the Huntington League.

Since no treatment or cure for Huntington's Disease is known, the project concentrated on preventive action. It aimed at primary prevention: to prevent, in a voluntary way, the spread of the disease; secondary prevention: to prevent late detection or treatment or no detection and treatment at all in actual victims; and tertiary prevention: to prevent additional handicaps such as depression, premature loss of work and social stigma.

Simple as it might seem, a population is needed to do research and to develop self-help groups. This is not so simple in the case of Huntington's Disease where people hide because of the fear of social stigma. Using data collected previously by hospital-based Huntington's Disease physicians, the project researchers (a social nurse and a social worker) started to visit the families at home. During these introductory visits, the researchers tried to reconstruct family trees. To date, 165 different pedigree families are known, of which the family tree has been completely reconstructed in 86 families. This indicates that the disease is probably more widespread than the scarce epidemiological data suggests. During the visits, the families were also informed of the existence and the activities of the Huntington League and their collaboration in research was requested. After the visits, informative letters on the activities of the Huntington League were sent to them.

Initially these home visits took place in two regions. The regions were selected for two reasons: (1) the prevalence of cases and (2) the availability of central group members who could help to start new groups. Soon after the first home visits, the regional groups started, this being indicative of the need and willingness of those contacted to discuss their - hitherto hidden - problems. So this personal and active approach, though opposed by many as an invasion of privacy, seems to have worked. Even those who did not want to become members of the Huntington League enjoyed talking to a 'sympathetic listener' and agreed to collaborate in research.

It was decided that a comprehensive study of the social consequences of the disease would be needed to persuade politicians to promote more services and programmes. From the list of known potential victims, a random sample of fifty families with an ill person and fifty families with a person at risk was selected. A separate questionnaire was constructed for each group. Besides medical data, the questionnaire for patients tried to collect information about the psychosocial and economic repercussions of the disease on the family. The questionnaire for families at risk concentrated on the knowledge of hereditary problems and on the coping mechanisms developed by these families. At the moment the data on patients and potential sufferers are being computer-processed; the analysis and reporting on patients will soon be ready.

Some findings already available from the first analysis indicate that the extent of the problem is broader than ever imagined. For example, professionals as well as families show an immense lack of information on the disease, so that the period between the onset of the disease and the first symptoms on the one hand, and the final diagnosis on the other hand, averages about eight years. One-tenth of the patients even died without having been diagnosed. It takes little imagination to see how these patients have been 'treated'. Another striking finding is the reported loss of social activities and social contacts, due to social stigma inherent in the hereditary aspect of the disease and the public's disapproval, arising from the involuntary movements which are often misinterpreted as a sign of alcohol intoxication.

Families lack knowledge about heredity. Moreover, topics like anti-conception, birth-control and abortion are very controversial in Belgium (a country with an influential majority of the population adhering to catholic values). In the self-help groups however, problems and possible solutions are freely discussed, so that people can make personal choices. In this way primary prevention can be brought about. Information about available services and emotional support in groups contributes to tertiary prevention. And finally, the League's ambition to inform professional health workers should bring about secondary prevention.

Actual functioning

The Huntington League obtained legal status as an independent non-profit making organisation. Rather than discussing the implications of this legal form, a clearer picture may be gained from a description of the present components of this organisation.

In the two regions, every few months, the livingroom-groups meet with an average of about twenty-five persons per meeting. Here, information is exchanged, emotional support given and possible solutions to problems are proposed.

A small group edits a three-monthly newsletter that is sent out to all members. This newsletter is a way of maintaining contact with those people who do not attend the meetings. This group also produces special issues. A plan for the near future is the publication of an informative booklet to be sent to all medical doctors in Flanders.

The scientific advisory committee forms an essential part of the League. It brings together professors in human genetics, neuropathology, neuropsychiatry and psychotherapists. This board provides services for individual members and is also actively engaged in planning activities of the Huntington League.

As pointed out above, the researchers also function in their roles of social nurse and social worker. They also act as a central and easily indentifiable point of reference by answering letters and phone calls from individual members. They are also active in assisting the local groups.

The executive group consists of three members directly involved with Huntington's Disease and one volunteer; this group also functions as a formal board of directors. They take care of financial and organisational problems, facilitate the functioning of the Huntington League and execute decisions taken in the core group. They meet at least once a month, but if needed, every week.

The most central body or 'heart' of the League is the core group. Besides the members of the executive group, it consists of representatives of: the two regional groups, the editorial board and the scientific advisory board. They centralise information, clarify needs and desires and plan activities.

These bodies serve one hundred and fifty active members and their families and all those concerned with Huntington's Disease. This not only includes emotional support, social activities, information and education, but also the provision of direct services, research activities and social and health policy making.

Relations with professionals

The Huntington League presents a special case in that lay people and professionals have collaborated closely from the beginning. This close collaboration is not only based on goodwill but also simple necessity. The afflicted depend on medical professionals for palliative care, hospitalisation and the eventual detection and development of a treatment. On the other hand, medical doctors who want to do scientific research on Huntington's Disease need a population for their experiments for the development of predictive tests and the trying-out of new medication for example. Huntington's patients and people at risk are eager to participate in these medical experiments since their success might be the solution to the basic problem.

This mutually beneficial relationship between lay people and professionals does not of course exclude the existence of humanitarian motives on the side of the professionals. They understand that, rather than a definite cure, daily care for the patient is crucial.

In the literature on self-help a controversy exists about whether groups are started by lay people or professionals. The Belgian Huntington League is an example of how a professional was introduced by American lay-initiative and stimulated Belgian lay people to do the same.

Broadening the scope

The existence of Huntington Leagues has not been restricted to the U.S.A. and Belgium. In many other countries like the Netherlands, Great Britain, Canada and Australia, groups have started and developed initiatives. These groups collaborate internationally. During the fourth meeting of representatives of the existing groups, held in Leuven in October 1981, the International Huntington Association (IHA) was founded. The IHA is a federation of national voluntary health organisations and self-help groups concerned with Huntington's Disease. It aims at supporting the national groups in their main activities and will assist in the development of Huntington's Disease groups in other countries. One immediate goal is to start a Huntington League in

Italy, France and Germany. The IHA also plans to co-operate with other voluntary health associations in order to influence international policy-formulating bodies like the World Health Organization.

IHA brings together national Huntington Associations but does not want to restrict itself to Huntington's Disease. Huntington's Disease has hereditary, neurological and physically handicapping aspects. Every advance in the field of heredity, neurology and care for the handicapped, is considered to be a contribution to the solution of Huntington's Disease. Therefore the IHA wants to collaborate with other associations or groups active in any of these three fields. So the general principle of self-help - 'people actively engaged in solving their problems together' - is not only active at the level of the individual patients meeting in local groups, but also at the level of the organisations meeting internationally.

Note
This article was written in collaboration with Andrea Boogaerts (social nurse), Trees Cloostermans (social worker), Jan Deroover (neuropsychiatrist) and Miet Wouters (volunteer), all active members of the Belgian Huntington League.

A WOMEN'S DISPENSARY
Christiane Viedma

A cold day in December. The snow has fallen early this season and a thin white layer covers the roofs of Geneva, the small Swiss city where the World Health Organization has its headquarters.

Not far from where the lights of luxury hotels are reflected in the peaceful waters of Lake Geneva, their lobbies thronged with international visitors, there is a curious district which is called the people's quarter, no doubt because a large proportion of its inhabitants belong to the least favoured section of the city's population; old people with low incomes, immigrant workers and so on. This is also the area where prostitutes wait for potential clients.

In one narrow little street, the fourth house has a notice on its very ordinary door which reads: Women's Dispensary.

The door opens to my knock, and I am plunged into a cheerful, bustling and welcoming scene. A small child sits in a push-chair. The room is simple, well-lit and friendly. As I hang up my coat, I wonder which are the doctors or nurses and which the patients, since nobody wears a white gown.

A member of the dispensary staff, Mrs Rosangela Gramoni, guides me through to an adjoining apartment whose bedrooms have been transformed into gynaecological and paediatric consulting rooms, and the living-room into a meeting hall.

I ask where the usual gynaecological examination chairs are. Mrs Gramoni smiles and say: 'You see, we only have one for very special examinations and for inserting intra-uterine devices. Otherwise all examinations are done on an ordinary bed'. In fact I had noticed in each room a divan covered with coloured towelling cloth and a few flowered cushions. On a small table lie a number of instruments, plastic gloves and three objects - a speculum used for vaginal examinations, a hand-mirror and a pocket torch. Observing my interest, Mrs. Gramoni explains: 'These are our basic instruments. Most women apply the speculum themselves. It is made of soft plastic and causes no discomfort. Then we give them the mirror and the torch so they can see the neck of their own uterus'. From the way she lined up these objects on the table, it was clear that they were somehow symbolic of a new approach to gynaecological health care.

She added: 'But come and see the gynaecological chair you asked about; after all, we do use it occasionally'. And there it was,

134

a chair just as one sees in the consulting rooms of any gynaecologist or in an obstetric ward. What was different was that the 'stirrups' were covered with a hood of flowered tissues and the metal bars with a knitted sleeve, 'because those bars are so cold'. Pinned to the ceiling was a poster with a pleasant country scene 'so that the user in the chair doesn't get bored during the examination or operation'.

'You said the user?'

'Yes, the word 'patient' suggests that the person consulting these services receives the services passively without always understanding them. But we consider our services as an exchange. All we are doing is to teach the women who live here what we know, and we too are permanently 'under training' in the course of our work. I myself am a biologist, and I learnt here how to carry out a test for possible cancer of the cervix, or do a pregnancy test. Thanks to our users, we are also trying to build up a new type of health care, more accessible and more human. At all costs we try to avoid creating a hierachical relationship with those who come here. That is why we don't wear white gowns, which would set a distance between us and would become a symbol of authority. What we want is to break the traditional expert-versus-patient relationship'.

This trend is exactly along the lines observed by Ilona Kickbusch, a sociologist working as a consultant with WHO's European Regional Office in Copenhagen. Where for decades the doctor treated and the patient complied, she now observes a new relationship - 'an exchange model based on a service economy: the doctor is termed the provider of health care and the patient the consumer - and it is up to the consumer to cooperate with the provider to ensure optimum results.'

It is certainly true that in any industrialised country it is difficult to imagine a health worker without a white gown, which is supposed to be essential for good hygiene. Fully aware of this, the workers at the Dispensary have twice asked the hygiene service of the City of Geneva to inspect the premises and the clothing worn; no pathological agent was detected. 'I think it may be the first time an establishment has actually made such a request', one of the staff commented.

This unconventional dispensary has been in existence since May 1978. But it all started a year and a half earlier when a nurse at a city hospital, dissatisfied with the small amount of time she could devote to each patient and with the impersonal way in which she often had to treat them, wrote to several women of the city inviting them to start a discussion group.

For eighteen months, seventeen women used to meet once a week and these preliminary meetings resulted in 1978 in the setting up of a non-profit-making foundation, entirely administered by its own staff. Later, three doctors - all of them women - joined the enterprise. The other workers have various backgrounds and come not just from the health professions, like the nurses and midwives, but from other fields: they include a biologist, a psychologist, a teacher, an interpreter, and an occupational therapist.

'The fact that the doctors arrived only after the dispensary had started is in my view very important', says Mrs Gramoni, 'because it enabled us from the outset to overcome the bad habits learned during medical training or during hospital work. I should add that our doctors are very remarkable women. They have to be remarkable to join a dispensary already in working order and to receive the same salary as other workers who have not had the same training as they have.'

The staff participation aspect operates on a completely egalitarian basis. Each of the fourteen workers who form the staff takes turns in carrying out every duty, whatever her training: reception, administrative work, maintenance, health education and preventive work. And they are all paid at an equal rate of fifteen Swiss francs an hour - the equivalent of an untrained manual worker or a cleaning woman. Monthly earnings only vary according to the hours put in at the dispensary, which in any case do not exceed a half day. The workers want to offer everyone who comes a fair hearing and really personal attention, both of which would be incompatible with long and harassed working hours.

Financially, the dispensary's situation is precarious. It was started thanks to donations and for the past two years has received an annual subsidy from the City of Geneva. But the subsidy it requested from the Canton of Geneva has just been refused and it faces a deficit, with revenues only just sufficing to cover salaries. The revenues are very limited since most of the users are among the lowest income groups and are therefore entitled to the minimum tariff scale for medical treatment.

The dispensary already has two thousand case-histories and does not accept new users unless they are especially under-privileged women with social or sexual problems. These numbers and the regularity of attendance are sufficient proof that the dispensary responds to a real social need, but it cannot expand for fear of falling into the same difficulties as the overburdened health services and of failing, like them, to offer the care that is needed.

'But if we cannot expand, at least we can multiply', says Mrs Gramoni. 'That is our philosophy, and I believe firmly that the future of the dispensary is that of many dispensaries'. Preparatory work on similar clinics is under way elsewhere in Switzerland, and in Geneva itself there is talk of a Dispensary Number 2. Comparable places already exist in Western Europe and North America.

Each week the staff at the dispensary hold an administrative meeting and, every three months, the users themselves are invited to an assembly. Fully ten per cent of the users attend - quite a high participation for an urban population in a highly industrialised country. They discuss the running of the dispensary, and the criticisms and suggestions made during this 'community participation' often have a direct effect on its activities. 'In fact, this assembly has become their own', says Mrs Gramoni. 'At first, we spoke and the users replied. Nowadays we scarcely intervene at all and the discussions take place among the users.'

Consultations

A consultation at the dispensary could be defined as the application of a new kind of medicine in which no visit is rushed through in ten minutes on the pretext that time is too short. The role of receptionist is considered as a key one, which each of the workers undertakes in turn. It involves answering all manner of queries by telephone, which calls for an excellent knowledge of all the problems that may arise and of all the solutions available to the dispensary.

It also involves making the first and most important contact between the user and the dispensary. The problem, the anxiety, the disease which brings the user there is not dealt with in an isolated way. Each individual is considered in her social, marital and environmental context, in everything that may directly affect her health to a large or small degree. So it is important from the first visit that the dispensary workers should obtain a precise picture of the user's situation and start to build up an atmosphere of confidence which alone can encourage the user to take charge of her own health.

The user begins by filling in a very full questionnaire on her medical and gynaecological history - her periods, whether she has had children, what method of contraception she uses. Then two of the workers discuss the replies with the user and explain the purpose of the preventive gynaecological examination which she will have.

This begins with palpation of the breasts as a first check for cancer. The woman is shown how to make this examination herself, its importance is explained to her, and she learns how to distinguish the alarm signals. If a suspicious lump shows up, she is referred to a gynaecological polyclinic which will look after her case. Next comes the palpation of her abdomen, as a check that her digestion is normal. A urine analysis is made and her blood pressure is measured. Finally, a vaginal examination. At this stage the user is given the speculum and is told how to place it herself. With the mirror and the pocket torch she can observe her own genital organs and the neck of the uterus. A sample of vaginal secretions is made as a check against infection and a swab is taken as a check against cervical cancer. The woman is encouraged to obtain a speculum herself and to make a regular inspection at home so as to be aware of any change that might suggest an anomaly.

After the first examination, the user may choose between the standard treatment practised by all gynaecological services, or treatment by 'alternative medicine', rather as a patient who goes to hospital in China can choose between the department of 'Western' medicine or the deparment of traditional Chinese medicine, where treatment by acupuncture or medicinal herbs is available.

An 'alternative' treatment exists for most gynaecological problems. Thus, if the bacterial flora of the vagina has been destroyed following a decline in the woman's general condition or through taking antibiotics, with a resulting case of vaginitis, the bacteria can be reconstituted by the application of lactoferments such as are used in making yoghurt. A cystitis which has resisted several months of treatment with antibiotics was cured in a matter of weeks by drinking three litres of liquid each day in the form of an infusion of different herbs. One user explains that she successfully cured a case of trichomoniasis by the use of clove of garlic. The use of other herbs such as artemisia, parsley or pennyroyal has proved effective in remedying late periods.

But treatment is not everything at the dispensary, which also deals with requests for abortion, oversees the progress of pregnancies and some births, and advises on family planning, arranging discussion groups on contraception, child care, menopause problems and so forth in which non-users can take part. The dispensary itself does not carry out abortions, but directs women who ask for one towards the appropriate public service which offers a therapeutic abortion covered by the health insurance system. A dispensary workers goes along with the user to help with these arrangements if required.

The dispensary offers any family who wants it - provided home conditions are good - a delivery at home with the assistance either of a dispensary midwife or one from the city services. As often as possible, fathers too are associated with these activities. They are invited to the preparatory sessions before a delivery - which include psychological preparation for the birth, physical exercises and relaxation and they may even play an active role. 'I can quote you an example of a father who cut the umbilical cord himself', says Mrs Gramoni. After a home delivery, mother and child are observed every day for ten days, and the dispensary offers advice on paediatric care.

Primary health care

Although the dispensary practises secondary prevention, that is to say the early diagnosis of an already existing disease, its interest first and foremost is in primary prevention, which can in itself effectively combat the alarming rise in the cost of health services. This simply means preventing people from falling ill by recommending better nutrition, better hygiene in their daily lives, and better working conditions.

recommending better nutrition, better hygiene in their daily lives, and better working conditions.

'If it is true what the experts say, that sixty to seventy per cent of cancers are of environmental origin', comments Mrs Gramoni, 'prevention ought to be applied to the environment itself rather than stopping short at early diagnosis. What is needed is to teach people how to stay in good health and that is something that cannot be done without their active participation. It is at that stage that the activities of our Women's Dispensary fall within the definition of primary health care.

This definition is clearly not quite the same thing that applies in the countries of the Third World, since the situation is quite different in the industrialised countries. But there is a close parallel in the need for members of the community themselves to participate in health. This is becoming more and more apparent in a Western European country like Switzerland. This is a current which forms part of the much broader ecological trend. In view of the enormous demand from the population of Geneva, it is clear that the more humane and less 'medical' approach to health care offered by this dispensary, with its accent on prevention, is giving many women satisfaction, responds to a great need, and suggests a starting point for solving the crisis in the world's health care systems.

Note. This article appeared originally in World Health

SHORT-TERM AND LONG-TERM EFFECTS OF LAY GROUPS ON WEIGHT REDUCTION

A. Grimsmo, G. Helgesen and C. Borchgrevink

Introduction

Obesity is a growing health problem. Although only severe obesity is related to excess mortality (Garrow,1979), increase in morbidity seems to affect people who are only 25 per cent overweight (James, 1978). Serious diseases such as diabetes, hypertension, gall stones and psychiatric disturbances are among the most common complications accompanying obesity. The treatment of obesity by doctors has largely failed (Karlsson et al, 1975). In Norway, as in several other countries, self-help organisations for weight control have recently sprung up. We describe the function and the results of one such organisation (Grete Roede Slim-Clubs).

Subjects and methods

During a five-year period self-help organisations for weight control have grown into a nationwide movement. Altogether eighty thousand people have participated. They work in small groups, usually from eight to twelve members, meeting once a week for eight weeks, and monitoring body weight each time. They are given a low-calorie diet, are encouraged to do physical exercise, and are strongly advised against alcohol. The cost of the course, 350 Norw Kroner, is paid in advance. The groups are led by non-professionals, usually women have who have participated in earlier courses themselves and who have succeeded in slimming. Although not formally organised, many members meet their 'hostess' once a month after the initial course as a type of continuous slimming programme. Members are recruited mainly by advertising in the local press and through the local grapevine.

Our study was carried out in three steps. Firstly, we carried out two prospective studies looking at the short-term effect of the weight reduction programme, one in a large group and the second in two small groups closely observed by one of us (GH). Through a retrospective survey we then studied the long-term results.

Secondly, to study the short-term effect, one of us joined two groups totalling 33 participants (all women) and followed them regularly for eight weeks, interviewing each person. Follow-up interviews were conducted after three, six and twelve months. In addition, we obtained data from all those who started the weight reduction course during the spring of 1977, including the initial weight, weight at weekly intervals, and the end result. The data were collected by the 'slim-club hostesses' and sent to us at the end of the course.

Finally, in the retrospective study of the long-term effects we carried out a two per cent structured sampling of all who had participated over the past five years. The slim-club hostesses throughout the country were given detailed instructions about the sampling procedure. They sent us the names, addresses, ages, heights, and weight results of 1,114 selected participants at the beginning and at the end of the course. All were sent a letter and questionnaire asking their present weight.

Results

Table 1 gives the results of weight reduction in the small group of 33 women who were closely followed by one of us. The average weight loss of 6.5 kg (range 3-10 kg) at the end of the course was followed by a further decrease of 1.2 kg after three months. The weight at six months was still lower than at the end of the course, but after one year there was an average gain of 1 kg compared with the weight at the end of the course. There was still, however, a weight reduction of 5.5 kg compared with the starting point.

Table 1: Short-term results and one year follow-up after an eight-week-long slimming-course (33 participants)

	At the course		Observation time		
	Weight at start	Weight at end	3 months	6 months	12 months
Mean weight (kg)	72.9	66.4	65.2	66.0	67.4
Minimun/maximum weight (kg)	57/89	53/81	53/82	51/86	53/84
Standard deviation	7.4	6.7	6.3	7.6	7.4

In the larger prospective study of short-term effects 11,410 people started the course and 10,650 (93.3 per cent) completed it, indicating that the programme was obviously well accepted. The average weight reduction for those who completed the course was 6.9 kg. Including the 6.7 per cent who dropped out, the average weight loss was 6.4 kg.

In the long-term study 1,114 people were sent a questionnaire; a reminder was sent to those who did not reply within two to three weeks. Altogether 948 (85.1 per cent) answered, which we consider most satisfactory. There were 95.5 per cent women and 4.5 per cent men, the average age was 38.5 years.

Table 2 gives the results. As the various courses during the year did not start at the same time, we have given the observation periods as one to two, two to three, or three to four years, rather than as two, three, or four years. The average weight remained fairly stable the first couple of years, but began to rise again after three to four years. At the end of the five-year period, on average subjects had regained about half of the weight they lost during the course, but were still 5-6 per cent below the starting point.

Table 2: Long-term results of weight reduction in an eight-week-long course

| | At the course | | Observation period (years) | | | | |
	Weight at start	Weight at start	Up to 1	1-2	2-3	3-4	4-5
Mean weight (kg)	79.5	70.0	69.8	69.5	71.3	72.1	75.4
Mean weight (% of initial weight)		88.4	87.8	88.9	90.8	90.5	93.6
Minimum/maximum weight (kg)	55/146	50/118	53/114	48/120	50/110	49/115	64/95
Standard deviation	13.0	10.5	11.3	11.0	10.2	11.5	10.0
No. of people observed	934		306	245	206	169	8

We may divide the participants into three groups according to the long-term results (Table 3).

Table 3:   Long-term results of weight reduction when divided into three groups according to success

Group*	Observation period (years)			
	Up to 1	1-2	2-3	3-4
I	2.6%	6.9%	13.1%	14.8%
II	31.1%	44.9%	47.6%	49.7%
III	66.3%	48.2%	39.3%	35.5%
Total	100%	100%	100%	100%
No. of persons	306	245	206	169

* See text for explanation

Group 1 - Those who had regained all or even more of the weight lost during the initial course. After one year 2.6 per cent belonged to this group; this increased to about 15 per cent after three to four years.

Group II - Those who had regained some, but not all, of the weight lost during the course. After one year about one-third belonged to this group and the figure increased to about half at the end of three to four years.

Group III - Those who had either maintained the reduced weight at the end of the course or were still losing weight. After one year two-thirds belonged to this group, but the figure was reduced to 35 per cent at the end of three to four years, which is still a remarkably high proportion. Even if the 15 percent who did not answer our questionnaire had regained all their weight the percentage belonging to group III would still be as high as 30.

Discussion

In collecting the data we had to rely heavily on collaboration with the slim-club hostesses. It would naturally be in their interest to obtain positive results, but in the methods used we have tried to eliminate this possible bias. In the large prospective short-term study we collected results from all participants without sampling. A record for each participant, including the initial weight, the weekly weight measurement, and the end result, was written in by the hostesses, but fully controlled by the participants themselves. Obtaining the same result both in the large and the small, carefully controlled, short-term study also strengthens the reliability. In the retrospective long-term study we made several spot tests and did not find any misunderstanding of the instructions sent to the hostesses. In one group of participants we did the sampling ourselves, and this group had the same results as the others. All in all, therefore, we think that the reliability was quite good.

In a study such as the present retrospective one there is always a possibility that the replies are not honest. We have not checked this, but we emphasised the importance of honesty in our letter to the participants. The questionnaires were returned anonymously to us and not through the hostess. Furthermore, the results after one year were similar in the retrospective study and in the controlled prospective study. All in all, we think that the answers were reliable.

Comparing a self-help organisation in England - TOPS (Take Off Pounds Sensibly) - and a group led by a behaviour therapist, Levitz and Stunkard stated in 1974: "We believe this is the clearest demonstration to date of the greater effectiveness of professional over non-professional therapeutic intervention." We disagree with this conclusion for two main reasons.

Firstly, we have shown that a lay organisation can be highly effective in helping people to lose weight. Looking at the results reached during the eight-week course, they are among the best we have been able to find (Table 4).

Table 4: Short-term results of weight reduction, comparing different studies

Author	Year	No. of subjects	Duration (weeks)	Treatment	Average weight loss (kg)
Stunkard et al	1980	24	24	Behaviour and medication	15.3
Jeffery et al	1978	108	20	Behaviour	5.8
Paulsen et al	1976	54	15	Behaviour and diet	8.4
Craddock	1969	76	8	Diet	2.7
Kingsley and Wilson	1977	78	8	Behaviour and diet	5.0
Present study	1977	10650	8	Behaviour and life style	6.9

The same probably also holds true for the long-term results, but here there are fewer studies to compare with. Feinstein (1960) analysed 161 articles on the management of obesity and concluded that on average 1-2 per cent of the people taking part in the weight-losing programmes maintained initial weight-loss for five years. Craddock (1969) surveyed eleven long-term studies and found that 1-13 per cent maintained some weight-loss for five years. These results along with more recent findings are shown in Table 5.

Table 5:   Long-term results of weight reduction, comparing different studies

Author	Long-term results		
Feinstein (1960)	1-2%	kept initial weight loss	5 years
Craddock (1969)	1-13%	kept some weight loss	5 years
Currey et al (1977)	30%	kept initial weight loss	1 year
Johnson and Drenick (1977)	7%	kept some weight loss	9 years
Hall (1973)	33%	kept initial weight loss	2 years
Present study	35%	kept initial weight loss	4 years

Secondly, when comparing professional and non-professional treatment of obesity, the number of participants should be taken into account. Participants in most studies published about professional treatment rarely exceed a hundred. We have studied over eighty thousand people during a five-year period. It would be almost impossible for the health-care system to cope with the problem.

The participants were in general not grossly overweight, but still they thought their weight was a problem that they wanted to do something about. In the small prospective study only about one-quarter had consulted a doctor beforehand because of obesity. We do not have corresponding figures for the two other studies.

Owing to the informal education and the wide latitude for personal initiative among the hostesses, it is not possible to give a detailed description of the actual work done during the eight weekly meetings. We have, however, tried to analyse the ingredients in the weight reduction programme.

Firstly, it is a popular movement built on self-help principles. It is made up and run by the obese individuals themselves. The hostesses have all been obese and have succeeded in losing weight in the same programme.

Secondly, they are organised in small groups. Mechanisms, such as group pressure, competition, and strengthening of self-consciousness play an important part.

Thirdly, the programme uses different reward systems, such as collecting points. The participants have to pay for the course in advance, so they are more likely to complete the course.

Fourthly, and finally, the programme also makes efforts to change the total life style, including changes in diet, more exercise, and reduced consumption of alcohol.

These findings have strengthened the conclusion found in recent reports about methods for treating obesity. The best results, both immediately and in the long run are reached by combining small groups, behaviour therapy, and intervention into diets and life styles. The study also indicates that combining scientific methods with lay work might provide a clue for solving serious health problems.

References

Craddock,D. (1969) Obesity and its Management; 2nd ed., Churchill Livingstone, Edinburgh.

Currey,H., Malcolm, R., Riddle, E., and Schachie, M., (1977) 'Behavioural treatment of obesity: limitations and results with the chronically obese', Journal of the American Medical Association, 237, 2829-31.

Feinstein,A.R. (1960) 'The treatment of obesity: an analysis of methods, results and factors which influence success', Journal of Chronic Diseases, 11, 349-92.

Garrow, J.S. (1979) 'Weight penalties', British Medical Journal, ii, 1171-2.

Hall, S.M. (1973) 'Behavioural treatment of obesity: a two-year follow-up', Behaviour, Research and Therapy, 11, 647-8.

James W.P.T. (1978) 'The prevalence and risks of obesity' in Why Obesity?, 22, suppl. 15, 15-26, Naringsforskning.

Jeffery, R.W., Vender, M. and Wing, R.R. (1978) 'Weight loss and behaviour change one year after behavioural treatment of obesity, Journal of Consulting Clinical Psychology, 46, 368-9.

Johnson, D. and Drenick, E.J. (1977) 'Therapeutic fasting in morbid obesity', Archives of Internal Medicine, 137, 1381-2.

Karlsson, Y., Halberg, K.K., Pelkonen, R., et al. (1975) 'Discussing obesity', Nordisk Medicin, 90, 145-53.

Kingsley, R.G. and Wilson, G.T. (1977) 'Behaviour therapy for obesity: a comparative investigation of long-term efficacy', Journal of Consulting Clinical Psychology, 45, 288-98.

Levitz, L.S. and Stunkard, A.J. (1974) 'A therapeutic coalition for obesity: behaviour modification and patient self-help', American Journal of Psychiatry, 131, 432-7.

Paulsen, B.K., Lutz, R.N. McReynolds, W.T., and Kohrs, M.B. (1976) 'Behaviour therapy for weight control: long-term results of two programmes with nutritionists as therapists', American Journal of Clinical Nutrition, 29, 880-8.

Stunkard, A.J., Craighhead, L.W., and O'Brian, R. (1980) 'Controlled trial of behavior therapy, pharmacotherapy, and their combination in the treatment of obesity, Lancet, ii, 1045-7.

Note: This article first appeared in the British Medical Journal for 24.10.81. Permission to republish is gratefully acknowledged.

ON IDENTIFICATION RESONANCE

Arno van der Avort and Pieter van Harberden

Researchers have paid little attention to the methods of helping used in self-help groups. In the literature on this subject, certain elements are often alluded to, but without making it clear whether these are specific to self-help groups. The universal operation of certain principles such as the helper therapy principle formulated by Reissman (1976) is often taken for granted. Hardly any attempts have been made to study in depth, to differentiate or to clarify the methods used in self-help groups. This paper explores one approach that is widely used - identification resonance.

The working of identification resonance

The process of 'identification resonance' starts when one or several members of the group present a certain aspect of a common problem and begin to talk of the feelings and personal experiences connected with it. Usually other members of the group recognise such feelings and experiences because they have already had the same experiences based on similar problems. Therefore, the members of the group identify with each other.

This mutual identification encourages each member, having heard what someone else has said about a certain aspect of the problem, to relate his own experiences. At first, similarities with what others have said appear, but soon the uniqueness of each person's situation becomes clear because every member of the group, from his own personal range of experience, adds something to what someone else has said. Each member of the group has unique personal associations with the situation.

These personal associations form the echo or 'resonance' of the mutual identification. This is why we speak of identification resonance. This resonance is essential for the therapeutic effect. It can be seen as extra information, and the therapeutic effect comes from the way in which one uses this extra information, which each individual member of the group did not have before taking part in the group session.

Through the resultant resonance, aspects of the central problem get a not previously discerned or completely different meaning for each member of the group. Thus a member of the group may find others have experienced the same aspects of a problem under similar or quite different conditions from his own situation; or certain common backgrounds may be discovered or

148

other similarities brought to light. Thus, an aspect of a problem gains meaning during the resonance process (through the associations in the group) and greater understanding of the problem is gained. New frames of meaning may even develop as more aspects of the problem are discussed through the identification resonance. This implies that many aspects of the problem will be clarified through an emerging resonance and more meaning and substance will be gained by all members of the group. The connections between the different aspects may also become clearer.

The therapeutic application of the identification resonance seems to be very extensive. First of all, the emerging identification and the associations that follow give more insight into the possible external manifestations of the problem or of certain aspects of the problem. Secondly, insight into the causes and backgrounds of the problem can be gained. And, thirdly, insight into possible solutions to the problem or to aspects of the problem can be offered. If, through the identification resonance a total perspective develops on the problem and on its many aspects and variations, it will contain insights into the external manifestations, the causes and backgrounds as well as some possible solutions.

From the life of a self-help group: an example of a session

Here we reconstruct three scenes from meetings of an AA group in which the members examine their problem situation, the causes and backgrounds of their problem and possible solutions. As we want to clarify the workings of the identification resonance, it is necessary to simplify the group process to some degree. In reality, interactions take place in a much more complex manner. Simplification enables us, however, to make the process clearly recognisable.

Our AA group consists of four people, two men and two women. They talk with each other about different aspects of their common problem - excessive use of alcohol. We indicate the different moments in the process of the identification resonance by means of short statements that have been put in brackets.

Scene 1:   Explanation of the Problem Situation

Victor: First of all, you are so powerless against it. The first thing you know is that you are drinking again. There are so many opportunities! This is what happened to me recently: at a party with acquaintances, the hostess offered me a glass of vermouth. I dared not refuse, because I was afraid of insulting her. And look, I slipped up again! Later I felt terribly miserable and guilty, but it had happened again.

Elsie: Well, I can easily believe that; I would have found it

149

difficult to refuse too (identification). But drinking alcohol is so normal; everyone joins in, so you have to. You can't escape (association - Elsie draws attention to the cultural pattern of drinking).

Adrian: The things you both say, I feel too (identification), but I think that it's only partly true. I feel in myself a need for drink, just like the need for food or sleep (association - as a result of what the others say, Adrian defines the alcohol problem not only differently but also more clearly; here the symbolic character of the process can be seen. Adrian interprets the problem differently from Victor and Elsie). It is not only a question of the many opportunities, but also of choosing to take them up. I know that I am just looking for opportunities to drink and can't resist opportunities (the association supplies a clear insight).

Marian: That's an important matter for all of us. We shouldn't shift the blame onto another or onto opportunities; we should consult ourselves. It is our problem; we do it ourselves. Alcohol is offered everywhere; it always comes back, but it is us that accept it! (Marian identifies with Adrian's opinions and reiterates them very clearly. This identification with Adrian's opinions makes his insight more dominant in the group. The emerging identification resonance has supplied a specific insight into the definition of the problem, with which the group continues the discussion).

Scene 2: Explanation of Causes and Backgrounds of the Problem
Adrian: Drinking alcohol is in fact only the expression of quite different and much deeper problems within ourselves.
Victor: I quite agree with you (identification). I think that we're too often inclined to consider the problem of excessive drinking separately. We then think that if we do not drink again our problems will be solved.
Marian: Yes, the issues at stake are actually our personal weaknesses and incompetence. These weaknesses of ours are the cause of our not being able to leave the liquor alone. Liquor has to divert our attention (here the identification leads to a clear association. Also, it is clear that a resonance develops gradually supplying specific insight; what is still vague and obscure with Adrian has been clearly formulated by Marian through Victor's remarks. The problem is put into perspective).
Elsie: So, we should take a kind of inventory of weaknesses and inabilities that we have and that cause our drinking. (The resonance becomes clearer and clearer: the problem is caused by weaknesses and inabilities not yet

150

defined which act as an immediate cause of excessive drinking.) This seems to me a good task for us all (the resonance even gives rise to the group's first self-activity: the tracing by every member of the group of the causes that exist within himself).

Scene 3: Explanation of Possible Solutions

Victor: Trying to improve myself is terribly difficult. I really do realise that I drink mainly because I am afraid to fail, at my work, in my family. But I don't know what to do about it. I see no way out. Whether I want it or not, the fear is there.

Marian Well, fear is something I know too! (Identification). Especially in situations that are unknown to me, that I've not experienced before (association). Then I'm terribly afraid that I'll say something wrong or that I'll behave stupidly. Every time I experience something like that I begin to drink. But the other day I was successful. I had to fill out some form that I had never seen before. At first, I felt very nervous and wanted to 'grab the bottle' so to speak. However, I was able to control myself, because I knew how miserable I would feel afterwards. Instead of drinking, I went to someone who could help me with the form (the association induces Marian to tell how she has been able to solve her problem at least once; this then begins to function as a stimulus to a more general solution).

Elsie: How good of you! I have also experienced something like that myself (identification). You see, I always begin to drink when I'm not immediately successful (association). But now I have succeeded several times in keeping off the bottle by taking my time over the things I have to do and by figuring out how best to do the job. True, I'm not yet successful at every task, but to be honest, I'm rather proud of those few times I've succeeded. (Up to now the identification resonance has given two possible stimuli to a solution, although they are still very specific. Adrian extends the line of thought and comes up with an important insight).

Adrian Now that I'm thinking about what you've said, I believe that the most important thing for us is not to stand still, remain passive or let ourselves be overwhelmed by negative feelings about ourselves. We must act, and work on ourselves, have the courage to learn and to do. (Adrian's association supplies a generalisation of the resonance that appeared and results in a general proposal for the solution of the alcohol question).

151

Conclusion

Identification resonance is a particularly forceful and effective way of helping people in distress. It enables members who have joined a group in a state of distress to draw on their own self-healing powers. This is sufficient to justify the right of self-help groups to exist.

Reference

Riessman F., in a special issue of <u>Social Policy</u> on self-help, Vol. 7, 1976.

NOTTINGHAM SELF-HELP GROUPS PROJECT: THE FIRST YEAR'S WORK
Judy Wilson

Introduction

The Nottingham Self-Help Groups Project was set up in the belief that self-help groups need and welcome support and resources and, with these, could increase both in number and effectiveness. At the end of the first year's work, we are here setting out our achievements so far.

A simple definition of self-help groups is:

"Groups of people who feel they have a common problem and have joined together to do something about it". (Richardson and Goodman, 1983)

The problems facing the groups with which this project is working are usually health problems, but also include social and personal issues. We recognise that there are many other types of self-help groups, for example in the employment field, but this project does not attempt to widen its scope to include them. Nor does it have close links with groups concerned solely with "self-care", though for some groups this becomes part of their work. The term mutual aid is also used in this report: it is just another way of describing the organisations and is used interchangeably with the term 'self-help'.

Nottingham is situated in the English Midlands and has a population of 300,000. Staff of the Nottingham Council for Voluntary Service (NCVS) pioneered work in this field, from 1975. Joint meetings of groups and professional workers were held annually from 1977-1980. This relatively small input began to illustrate the need for support and resources in this area of work, and it also showed it might have national significance.

In October 1980 the idea was mooted with the then Area Health Authority of funding for a special development project. After a consultation exercise and further discussions, the Health Authority agreed to support a small scheme, employing a part-time worker for 20 hours and secretarial help for the same time. The Community Health Council (CHC), which had given great support to this idea from the beginning, offered office space and equipment. A budget of £11,000 p.a. was agreed, with the money allocated from joint financing, initially for two years. The project began in January 1982, with Judy Wilson as project worker, based in the first floor offices at 54 The Ropewalk, the CHC offices, very near the General Hospital.

Though away from the main base of the NCVS, the scheme is managed by NCVS who are responsible for its work and deal with all financial matters. In addition a small advisory committee meets quarterly, receives reports on the work and acts as a sounding board. Its members include people from two self-help groups, the CHC, the Health Education Department and the University Medical School. Its chairman is deputy administrator at the General Hospital.

One of the functions of the project, that of monitoring and writing up its work, is being carried out with the support of Loughborough University, in particular with the help of Adrian Webb, Professor of Social Administration. His interest and support also comes from his role as Chairman of the Volunteer Centre, on whose board Judy Wilson serves as a co-opted member.

The objectives of the project when it began, were agreed as follows:-

(i)   To encourage and support the growth of new groups in the Nottingham area.

(ii)   To provide a range of services for groups to draw on, available to both new and established groups, e.g. typing, duplicating, meeting room, contact address, information on publicity etc.

(iii)   To provide an information service on the work of groups, both locally and nationally, to be available to workers in the health and social services, both voluntary and statutory.

(iv)   To promote knowledge and understanding about self-help among workers in the health and social services.

(v)   To spread information and ideas about self-help and how to make it effective, between self-help groups in the Nottingham area.

(vi)   To monitor and write up the work of the project in a way that is suitable for national and international circulation.

This report looks at each of these objectives in turn and sees how far each has been realised.

New Groups

When setting up a new resource it is difficult to know what use will be made of it, how much to publicise its existence and in what way. Production of a leaflet written in simple terms was one of the first objectives, in addition to, of course, setting up the office and employing a secretary. But even before it had been produced and distributed, people were contacting us for help with new groups. Before the office had been open a month, we had been asked for help in starting a new group for burns patients and their relatives by a sister at the City Hospital Burns Unit, and for advice on setting up a national organisation for sufferers of Myositis

Ossificians Progressiva, a rare and very disabling condition. By the end of 1982, a further 16 people - that is a total of 18 in all - had approached us for help. The speed at which the project has become known may well relate to the fact that the worker was already well known through her previous work at NCVS.

Some of these request have come to nothing - people used us to try out ideas and then changed their minds; other people found they needed to think the idea through for a very long time and may well start groups later on; in only one case was it felt that support was not appropriate, partly because needs were already being met by existing groups. Eight groups have however been established. Four further ones are likely to start in 1983 and people are still considering whether to start in a further three cases.

The problems on which these new groups were based were: partial sight, asthma, burns, premenstrual problems (two groups), coming off tranquillisers, handicapped children and Alzheimer's disease.

Would these eight groups have started anyway? In some cases, certainly they would have done. But in the majority of cases, we think that the group would either not have started at all, or would not have got through the initial setting up period easily. It is interesting to note that the two groups whose growth has been enabled by professionals, rather than started immediately by the people with the problem themselves, said they would not have got going without the project's intervention. Our experience is that a majority of people involved in starting groups have not done anything like this before - and the requests for support come from professional workers as much as from "sufferers" themselves.

The scheme has not been going long enough to know for how long people want to go on having support. Our guess is that it will vary enormously. What seems important however is to build up a friendly, informal relationship from the beginning, so that the group can return to the project for services and support later in its development, if it so wishes. This unstructured relationship is perhaps at the core of the project's relationship with all groups: it is not a co-ordinating body, nor can it be or should it be responsible for the work of groups. It is a resource which people can make use of as and when they wish. To be particularly useful however, our experience suggests that it is important to be involved at the very beginning of a group's existence in order to help them begin work on a sound basis. With mutual aid groups, it appears to be crucial, even more than other voluntary groups, to get the formula right as you start.

We have sometimes been asked to justify our existence when national organisations already provide back-up for their new branches. In these 18 requests, only 4 however were in fact local branches of national bodies. None of them received any significant amount of support and in one case the secretary was scathing about the lack of it. Few national organisations, to be fair, employ more than even one member of staff to help local branches and many have none. Our policy is to avoid duplicating the often very useful help national bodies give, and to keep good lines of communication open with them. So far this seems to have been successful. In some cases, the national bodies have expressed gratitude for our locally based service and voiced the feeling that other areas of the country could benefit from similar back-up.

This section ends with a few comments from people who have themselves started groups

"What you do is to help us help ourselves".

"I hadn't a clue. I didn't think it would work - then you came along."

"You have a clear role in helping to start the group, in explaining what self-help groups can do and feeding in ideas that might be appropriate for that particular group."

The quantity of work with new groups has been far greater than we anticipated when we began. While some financial help has usually been welcome, much more appreciated have been the practical services, the advice and the opportunity to use the project as a sounding board. In all these ways, we feel we have enabled the start of these groups without taking them over - a crucial point to be remembered by everyone who wants to support self-help.

Existing Groups

From the work at NCVS prior to 1982, we knew that some services would be needed by existing groups, even those of quite long standing. Certain of these we built into the project when it began - secretarial services and knowledge about meeting rooms for example. Other services have developed either as requests have been made: advice on appointing a paid worker; or as resources have become available: a volunteer who does posters.

Table I illustrates the type of help given to individual groups. In order to respect the groups' need for confidentiality we have not identified the groups.

Groups have a membership ranging from 12 to 200; have been going for one to fifteen years; cover problems relating to parenthood, bereavement, physical handicap, mental health problems and serious illnesses. There is no easy definition of self-help, as seen in the introduction and to attempt to draw too tight a boundary round it would probably be counter-productive.

A significant number of established self-help groups need and draw on resources once these are available. They appreciate the increased credibility that the project has given them and in some cases are beginning to widen the scope of their activity following contact with the project. The project must be careful however not to claim too much for its support for the work of the groups; it is important that the members themselves should have the credit.

Table I Help given to existing groups – Jan 1st-Oct 31st 1982

Group	Typing duplicating & posters	Advice on meeting rooms	Advice on structure of group	Advice on appointing a paid worker	Advice on fund-raising	Visit to meeting	Increased links with professionals	Student placements
1		×	×	×	×		×	
2		×	×					
3		×	×					
4			×					
5			×					
6				×		×		
7	×	×				×		
8	×							
9	×							
10	×	×						
11		×	×			×		
12						×		
13						×		
14	×	×	×			×		×
15						×		
16			×			×	×	×
17					×		×	
18						×		
19			×	×		×		
20					×			
21			×			×		×
22								
22	4	7	10	3	3	11	3	3

157

Nottingham Self-help Groups Project

Information

An article published in the <u>Guardian</u> in April 1982 attacked self-help groups for their lack of standards and for often not letting people know where they can be contacted. To accuse in this way is not productive, but it is true that groups come and go, secretaries change, meeting venues alter. With this in mind, one of the first tasks of the project was to provide an information service about the groups.

A duplicated directory was produced in March and 700 copies were sold (at 15p) to libraries, professionals and voluntary bodies. Partly because we ran out and partly because information changed so much, we published a better, printed version in October, helped much by the work of volunteers and an anonymous donation from a firm. 1500 copies were produced this time and have been distributed free to workers in the health service, using centralised networks for distribution like the Family Practitioner Committee. Libraries and other bodies have proved willing to buy a second edition which we kept at 15p. Marketing such a directory does however take time and skill and we are aware that we need to build this aspect into our information work, just as much as collating the information.

Groups proved to be enormously helpful in supplying us with information and welcomed this complementary way of publicising their existence. It is important to us that it <u>is</u> complementary and does not replace the groups' work of producing information about themselves and their work. The recipients of the directory welcome it too. Whether the number of referrals has increased or not is not known, but one would hope this to be the case. Two additional forms of information work have been undertaken. The first is to tell individuals who phone or call at our office about individual groups. Lately the number of enquiries has averaged 15 a month. This is not a service that has been widely advertised however, partly because of the pressures on a small staff. The second avenue for information has been through a monthly column in the <u>Nottingham Evening Post</u>: an idea suggested by members of groups themselves at one of our joint meetings, which are described later in this report. Since October, a column entitled "Self Help for Health" has been published, which includes a short account of one individual group and a photograph, a monthly diary of meetings and details of the directory.

A centralised source of information appears to be much welcomed by professionals and supported by groups. It is time consuming to provide accurately and not a simple service to maintain. The help of skilled volunteers has been crucial to the project in this particular aspect of its work, which needs to be further developed.

Contact with Professionals

It may seem repetitive when we say that the situation concerning professional workers varies enormously between groups, but as with some of the situations described earlier, there is great variation. From the groups' viewpoint, some prefer to be entirely autonomous and have no wish to build bridges with professionals. This is understandable when a group has evolved from a feeling that professional care has not solved their problems. Research is much needed into this whole area. However our experience so far is that a majority of groups wish to work with, rather than separately from, professionals. They feel, though, that health and social service workers do not know enough about them, let alone how to devise a partnership.

The project has made a small start in promoting knowledge about self-help. The directories have been a useful tool, but solve only part of the problem. The project worker has given nine talks to professional workers, including social workers and G.P.s. One of these was a joint talk by herself and members of two groups. Our feeling is that this must be the way forward - a joint approach by the project and groups. A scheme is being planned for 1983 which will help develop a pattern of joint talks.

During 1982, Nottingham changed to being a District Health Authority, and the disorganisation that inevitably accompanies reorganisation had its effects on developing links with professionals. Talks however were held with the District Medical Officer, the Nursing Officer and the Director of Nursing Services for the community, which laid good foundations for future developments of this side of the work.

Our initial conclusion is that many professionals are guarded in their support for self-help, but once they understand more about it, its strengths and its limitations, they are willing to develop links. Some individuals in Nottingham have been remarkable in the time and enthusiasm they have shown and credit must be given to them. In general however, this remains an area where considerably more needs to be done. Not only is it important to build up working relationships but also a climate of opinion among professionals which allows self-help to flower. Groups too need to learn more about the work of professionals and this was a topic at one of the six joint evening meetings held in 1982.

Bringing groups together

"Making self-help effective" and "Success stories": these were the themes for two series of joint meetings of groups held during the year. Both were a set of three meetings held at weekly intervals, the first being in June and July, the second in November. Attendance at each meeting ranged from 50-80 at the first series, to about 30 at each of the autumn set. Altogether 35 groups were represented at the meetings. Ten of these came to five or six of the total number of six meetings. 17 came to only one or two.

The first set of meetings covered practical topics:-
* Using the telephone
* Using the media
* Preparing and distributing publicity material

In each case a panel of outside "experts" and some members of groups gave short presentations, and the bulk of the evening was spent in small discussion groups. While the experts' (who included local journalists, public relations officers and printers) advice was welcome and mostly useful, what was particularly productive was the contributions from groups themselves, both as panel members and in discussion groups. It was clear that people were willing, actually really keen, to learn from each other despite the fact that their groups were based on such different problems. The amount of knowledge between them was great, but they were not always aware that they had this knowledge or confident that it was important enough to share. After the meeting on using the telephone, an information sheet was produced by the project worker.

As a result of the questionaires filled in by each person attending the summer meetings, the autumn meetings were planned differently. The format was the same, but the panel of speakers and many of the discussion group leaders were from groups themselves. Despite the lack of experience in speaking of some of them all gave excellent talks and managed to hide their nervousness.

The topics covered also came partly from the evaluation of the summer meetings. The angle this time was hearing how some groups had successfully tackled problem areas - an attempt to present and publicise good practice rather than give opportunities for complaint and despair.

Again, all subjects were crucial to the work of most groups:-
* Working with the medical profession
* Sharing the jobs round in a group
* Fund raising, especially getting other people to do it for you.

Though numbers were smaller, partly because of the time of year and the change of venue, the warmth of the meetings was very apparent. There was a definite feeling of enjoyment in each others' company and of identifying with other groups - in some ways a real feeling of a self-help movement.

As before, self-help members themselves are the ones to speak:-

"One of the great advantages of these meetngs is the opportunity we have to talk to members of other groups."

"It makes you feel you are not alone."

"I just like the getting together."

This side of the project's work has proved to be enormously valuable. The six meetings resulted in a real sharing of knowledge; in an increase in confidence; a first indication of a feeling of common identity; and an increase in the take up of other services of Nottingham Self-Help Groups Project.

Monitoring and publicising the project

This has always been one of our aims. To our knowledge, there is no identical project in Britain and yet a growing interest in the question of support to self-help. This report is intended as a contribution to the much needed increase in knowledge. The help of Loughborough University in supporting the monitoring is much appreciated. This is being done through the project worker's registration as a part-time research student.

Our feeling is that projects like this, whether called clearing houses, information centres or resource centres, are most effective on a local basis. The bulk of our time has been put into setting up a local resource for development in Nottingham, and we shall continue to do this.

It has proved rewarding however to take part in a national and international dialogue and despite the limitations of this small project, we shall continue to allocate a certain amount of time to contributing to this. However our project is not necessarily a blue-print. It is one way of providing backup for self-help on a local basis, which appears so far to have been reasonably successful. We hope that people elsewhere will be able to draw on our experience and use it where appropriate, but are not claiming ours as the one model to be adopted as it stands.

Community development

The skills of the worker and the basis for this project are very much those of community development. Our point of working begins from the belief that people can and want to contribute to their own community and to solving their own individual problems and those of people around them. There is in this a mixture of both altruism and selfishness. So far, there is much in common with neighbourhood and community work, and the development of organisations like playgroups and tenants groups. There is much in common too with the consumer movement. People don't want to be labelled as patients and clients - they want to help to define their problem and to contribute to solving it.

Self help groups have special needs. Their members are often people without much experience of running organisations; they often lack confidence in their own ability to contribute to groups; and the major health and social problems which face most of them make huge demands on their life, often making the time they have available for groups unpredictable as well as limited.

We combine realism about the limits of self-help groups with great admiration for all they achieve. This has proved to be a most exciting and rewarding year's work. Two aspects of it have proved to be particularly notable: the capacity local groups have to learn from each other and to undertake joint action; and the previously untapped potential that many people with problems have. With help and encouragement they can extend the work of self-help groups in partnership with professional workers.

Reference

Richardson, Ann and Goodman, Meg (1983) Self-help and Social Care: mutual aid organisations in practice. Policy Studies Institute, London.

HEALTH ENTERS GREEN PASTURES: THE HEALTH MOVEMENT IN THE FEDERAL REPUBLIC
Ellis Huber

There is a new and growing movement in the Federal Republic of Germany: the health movement. Its forms of organisation and aims are similar to the women's movement, the ecological and alternative movements and strong links have been developed between these movements.

The health movement first took shape at the 'Gesundheitstag 1980' in Berlin. The idea of calling such an alternative health congress arose in 1979 among a collective of critical health workers in Berlin who formulated the slogan 'a health congress not a docor's congress.' The Gesundheitstag was held at the same time as the 83rd German Medical Congress, known as the 'Doctors' Parliament'. Meetings of medical associations and professional organisations in Germany had not hitherto given rise to expressions of critical opinion or progressive ideas, or to a real exchange of views. As a result many doctors of both sexes, members of all the other professional groups that play a major part in public health care and social welfare, and above all members of the public, patients and people threatened by illness, felt that their interests were not being taken into account in the formulation of health policies by representatives of the medical profession.

The initiative for the 1980 Gesundheitstag came from people working in the health field who were convinced that there existed enough critical viewpoints, new ideas and practical proposals to break the monopoly over information and opinion held by the professional organisations and the makers of official health policy, and to bring alternative ideas to public attention. A call was sent out to 'everyone prepared to question their existing professional roles and to take an active part in reviewing the basic principles of medical and social practice', and it received an overwhelming response.

The 1980 Gesundheitstag became the basis for a completely new approach to health policy. Over 10,000 participants from all the health professions took part in discussions, seminars and working groups and in writing reports at this alternative medical congress. A new popular movement had grown out of ecological and feminist groups, voluntary organisations and other activities at the democratic grass-roots: patients could again have hope. The representative of the <u>Medical Tribune</u> appeared impressed:

'One positive aspect was the amount of attention given to self-help by patients, to health education and to consultations between patients and doctors. Another positive feature was theatrical presentations like the play by a group from Hamburg, in which a seriously handicapped patient defended his right to break off treatment. And a positive impression was given by the strong and convincing appeal for better, more humane care for those who in our system are always disadvantaged: the elderly, the mentally sick and the incurable ... There is no denying the force of this pioneering medical movement, whatever the problems it may encounter.'

One of those attending, the psychiatrist Franco Basaglia, spoke in the closing ceremony at Berlin's Deutschlandhalle: 'For a long time after the war ended I had prejudices against Germany. This conference has helped me to overcome them. I am excited: the Gesundheitstag is not over, it is just beginning'.

The documentation on all the themes and outcomes of the four-day Berlin meeting filled seven paper-back books, and led to the founding of a health publications company (Verlag Gesundheit). The Berlin health shop (Gesundheitsladen EV), which started off the Gesundheitstag and which acts as a clearing house for alternative health care and criticism, became the model for new health shops in more than 30 towns throughout the Federal Republic. These act as contact points and information centres for their regions. Through a number of inter-regional meetings, delegates from the health shops have since been trying to coordinate and develop a health care network for the Federal Republic, though without yet achieving a definite institutional form.

The regional health shops give an organisational basis for groupings of nurses, auxilliaries, social workers, doctors, psychologists, students, trainee health workers both professional and non-professional, and lay people aware of health problems. They offer a wide range of different kinds of working groups on every possible aspect of health and opportunities to obtain information on activities and new projects in the region. In addition, many of the health shops provide advice, offer facilities for patients and put people in touch with self-help groups whose work they support. Professional helpers find contacts for organising their own training courses, for instance in acupuncture or psycho-therapy, and have opportunities to take part in political action and discussion on health issues.

In Autumn 1981 the Hamburg health shop organised the second Gesundheitstag. As the foreword to the conference programme put it:

'We are coming together in Hamburg from all parts of the Federal Republic and from abroad. Our professional and personal situations are as different as our political affiliations. We are health workers from widely differing social contexts.

What links us together? As health workers and as patients we are affected daily by the present unhealthy situation whereby we are parties to the management of physical and mental suffering, to treating social problems as if they were psychiatric problems and to discrimination against and the exclusion of people on the fringes of society'.

'We have come together in groups in order to help each other and to protect ourselves against the 'expropriation of our health' and the regimentation of our lives. We work in trade unions, various political parties, health shops or other independent groups. We contradict the dominance of official medicine with a creative NO, because though ostensibly non-political it conceals, damps down and controls grievances and abuses. We differ from each other in our motivation for changing existing situations and in the alternatives we propose. These differences must remain, so that each one of us may retain his personal and political identity. We want to win back the capacity for discussion and cooperation in place of professional arrogance and competitiveness. ...'

'We refuse to add our new and alternative ideas to the useless prescriptions of our forefathers. We refuse to define health goals which would be generalised to apply to others. There are many kinds of health, just as there are many forms of beauty or happiness; in the same way there are many paths to health and various forms of resistance to whatever threatens it. We find our own way in our own everyday lives: we overcome the barriers and the competition between groups of professionals and the distance separating experts and lay people. We learn from each other and give each other mutual help'.

These passages reflect both the aims and the philosophy of the programme. Successes and problems, new ideas, new projects both finished and unfinished were all discussed, the main themes being the oppressed and rejected; health, environment and working conditions; work in the hospital; the health movement and politics; local health centres and domiciliary care; self-help and resistance; against psychiatry; old and new methods of healing; the health business; and vocational training.

'The Gesundheitstag is a working gathering, to be enjoyed and where health should be infectious!' This time 20,000 participants let themselves be infected, double the numbers at the first Gesundheitstag. The Hamburg meeting confirmed the continuity and the vigour of the movement, even if the technical problems of such a mass gathering often overwhelmed the 'self-help organisers', and the many facets of the programme made it difficult to define what was going on. Established, institutional medicine in the

Federal Republic was forced to take notice. Ideas and impulses from the health movement have begun to have a considerable influence on public discussion and official health policy.

It seemed important to continue activities at both regional and local levels in order to consolidate the movement. Hence the first Berlin Self-Help Conference held in December 1982. The invitation to it ran: 'Medicine is on the move, health care is changing. The health movement is awakening hopes and developing new approaches to practical health work. Health centre and domiciliary work and a variety of alternative projects offer health experts new ways of practising their profession and provide lay people with better methods of overcoming sickness and responding to their needs'.

This meeting was organised along the principles of the two previous Gesundheitstag in Berlin and Hamburg, but was explicitly confined to the region and was intended to influence local self-help policies and act as a forum for the growing regional health movement. It was organised by the Berlin health shop in less than four weeks, because the 50th conference of health ministers of the Lander, which was about to be held in Berlin, had chosen self-help as its main theme. As a result the conference was given headline treatment by the regional press. In the opening session the well-meaning, noncommittal resolution on self-help in health care agreed by the health ministers and senators of the Lander was read out and then sharply criticised. Even the two senators who had agreed to take part in a debate with representatives of the self-help movement gave only half-hearted support to the resolution.

A major success was gained when the Berlin Senate agreed to provide public support for alternative health projects, self-help groups and lay initiatives. In May 1983 the first state financed Self-help Contact and Information Centre in the Federal Republic was opened in Berlin: another will follow in 1984 in Hamburg. In July 1983 the Munich health shop is to organise the first Bavarian Gesundheitstag.

Developments since 1980 show an interesting pattern. As a first step the health movement had to show to itself and to the public that it existed and had a strong and large constituency. Then the movement went on to develop alternative structures, such as the health shops and the publishing company, so as to provide itself with a continuing voice. The second Gesundheitstag showed clearly that the movement was not just a single spasm but could mobilise even more participants and interest. This gave an impetus to projects more closely linked to established structures and to the pursuit of funding from established, public sources, for example for self-help clearing houses. Regionalisation has continued and instead of organising as in 1980 in parallel to the doctors' congress, in 1983 a strong opposition spoke up within the doctors' congress itself. Links are now being established with the representatives of the Green Party (Die Grunen) so as to develop a blueprint for a new type of public health policy and an 'ecology of health' for the Federal Republic.

With this development we are witnessing a unique process of formulating new approaches in health care through joint action on the part of users of the health care system and critical professionals in search of new forms of health care provision. To report on and review this development a third Gesundheitstag is planned for late 1984 or early 1985.

PART IV TOWARDS SUPPORTIVE POLICY

SELF-HELP: A NEW PERSPECTIVE FOR HEALTH CARE
Robert Lafaille

The welfare state is in a crisis and a number of its achievements are under review. A new ethos is needed to bring about a fresh start. In the health and social care context this means that a new conception of helping needs to be found. What is called the self-help movement does embody such a new conception of helping - an emancipatory ideal of liberty, directed against the often superfluous and, in many cases, dependency creating, professionalised form of helping.

From this perspective, man is allowed to take responsibility for his own fate in emergencies. First and foremost, he possesses internal strengths, self-healing powers and psychic defences. These internal strengths have not yet been fully clarified, partly due to the alienating character of our culture (a dualistic concept of man, rationalism, and so on); but, in the future, they will certainly be explored and developed (Roszak, 1978). In this connection, it is important that citizens should be given the means to make use of the power of self-help and that, in education, attention should be explicitly directed towards the development of these human powers. Of course, self-help is not a panacea for all the damaging side-effects of the welfare state. But it could be that the values that this movement brings to the fore will influence all fields of helping. It is even possible that the whole health system might be based on these values.

At the moment there are two manifestations of these new values: self-help groups and self-help techniques. This is not to say that no other manifestations ought to or will develop, but it is in these two forms that self-help has most clearly crystallised at the moment.

<u>Self-help groups</u> are groups of fellow-sufferers concerned with common problems (van Harberden and Lafaille, 1979a). Self-help groups form around very specific and concrete problems. The distress experienced is mainly of a non-material and psycho-social nature. Although numerous self-help groups form around a disease or handicap, this disease or handicap never stands alone: with self-help groups it is always connected with psycho-social factors like loneliness, fear, lack of understanding and stigmatisation. The self-help techniques used are: discussion of the problems, exchange of information and experience, personal awareness,

169

mutual support and encouragement. In self-help groups, fellow-sufferers learn from each other's experiences and from each other's knowledge. This knowledge comes from experience rather than from books or from the conventional 'authoritative' detached knowledge of experts.

Usually professionals take no part in these groups. (For the relationship between self-help groups and professionals, see van Harberden and Lafaille, 1979b.) In a large number of cases, the group has been founded by someone who has had to contend with the problem himself and has conquered it or has learned to live with it.

Self-help techniques are applied by individuals. By self-help techniques is meant a body of knowledge and skills together with the aids required to apply them, such as a sphygmomanometer or an instruction book, enabling the individual to solve his problems autonomously in the physical or psychic field without direct help from professionals. Indirect professional help cannot, of course, be excluded. This takes effect through several channels, for example education, information and the development of new technologies. Self-help techniques are directed at self-diagnosis and self-treatment. Self-medication is a somewhat older shoot on the stem of self-help techniques. A more recent trend has been the increased lay handling of medical instruments. It is not just a matter of the vaginal spectrum which has been filched, not without some self-congratulation, by feminists from GPs and gynaecologists. A renowned institution, the Netherlands Heart Foundation, recently announced the sale of sphygmomanometers on a national scale, with the intention of encouraging people to check their own blood pressure regularly. In the sphere of self-help groups, there is the example of the Diabetes Association of the Netherlands, which encourages the self-administration of insulin.

The development of self-help techniques

The market for self-help techniques is still almost completely open for exploitation. In contrast to self-help groups, a definite professional input would be necessary here. It could be argued, on ideological grounds, that it is immoral and dangerous for man 'to play at being doctor' if no adequate techniques are available. Thus, technology needs to be developed by scientific research, especially if one is to deter present day forms of 'quack' medicine such as the passing off of placebos for personal profit. It would be a catastrophe if the medical bastion were to be replaced by a bastion of quacks. Further, it would require considerable effort on the part of professional helpers to teach people to use these newly developed technologies. It is here that primary health care has an important part to play. In the long run this task can be dealt with by making health education an obligatory subject in school.

The following guidelines may be a starting point for the development of self-help techniques.

1. People should be left to do those things which they can reasonably do themselves. This is the way to maximise their own responsibility. The things that they can carry out for themselves ought to be extended as much as possible.

2. Those techniques which are naturally available to the individual are preferable. In particular, techniques involving the individual's own mind and body need to be maximised. Thus, breathing and relaxation exercises are preferable to medication in the case of insomnia.

3. More scope should be created for a group approach to health problems. Different forms of group approach are possible. There are the self-help groups already mentioned. There are also training groups in which medical information is given, or one or other medical technique is taught, such as heart resuscitation or first aid. Several subjects, like euthanasia or the support of dying people, lend themselves to the formation of discussion groups, through which participants can better form an opinion on these subjects.

4. Priority must be given to preventive as opposed to curative techniques. Correct breathing, posture, exercise and hygiene, healthy food, learning to live with emotions and tensions - in short, a healthy way of life - should have high priority.

5. It is important to look for specific self-help techniques in conjunction with a programme for a healthy way of life, for example yoga. Such a programme offers a framework for the individual to hold onto. Fragmentary information or ad hoc advice have no chance of being influential.

6. The suggested techniques must not involve large risks. Determination of the level of risk, by means of scientific research, is necessary.

7. High valuation should be given to the personal experiences and knowledge of the individual.

8. Fixation on one's body should be avoided. Excessive preoccupation with one's own disease may retard recovery and may also become a source of serious problems as in the case of the so-called 'neurotic complainer'. In order to avoid this pitfall, a new concept of disease can be found in the work of Bandler and Grinder (1981). These authors point to the fact that disease, in our culture, is usually looked upon as fate, something that happens to you; whereas it would be much better to consider disease as a friend. Disease is really a sign that something is wrong

       with your life. The challenge is to interpret this signal in
an adequate way. Learning to live with imperfections
should prevent one from having a fixation on one's own
body.

9. The development of self-help techniques should be
associated with a view of man that sees him as an integral
whole. Both the complaint and learning to live with the
complaint will then be treated as being on a par with each
other.

Two examples

Hyperventilation (Compernolle, 1981). Fits of terror are a
frequent phenomenon. Occasionally everybody experiences an
attack of terror in threatening circumstances. Some people,
however, suffer from continually recurring fits of terror. Their
frequency may vary from several times a month to several times a
day. These frequent fits of terror usually stem from
hyperventilation, which is the breathing out of too much carbon
dioxide. Breathing out too much carbon dioxide causes important
changes in the chemical make-up of the body. This is why a person
who hyperventilates often suffers a whole range of other problems.
This is not because he/she is a neurotic complainer; real objective
changes occur in the whole body. Estimates suggest that
approximately ten per cent of the population regularly suffer from
complaints that result from hyperventilation.

    The reasons why people begin to hyperventilate vary. One
may begin to hyperventilate because of incorrect breathing, but
also because of psychic factors. Usually it is a vicious circle:
hyperventilation creates fear and fear is or may be a cause of
hyperventilation. The main problem is to break the vicious circle.
The traditional treatment for hyperventilation has been
psychotherapy. This treatment has many disadvantages and
generally little effect. More sensible and much cheaper is to deal
with hyperventilation either by means of breathing techniques or
by bringing on an attack.

    The simplest method is learning good breathing techniques.
However, some people cannot be helped by improving their
breathing techniques. Hence a second method can be used -
bringing on an attack of hyperventilation. Dr. Theo Compernolle,
who has applied this technique for years in his clinical practice, has
developed the procedure into a self-help technique in the form of
programmed instructions. It appears to be quite practicable for
people to treat themselves in this way. Evidence so far shows that
in a great number of cases the fits of terror are kept at bay after
such treatment. So psychotherapeutic help is only considered in
those resistant cases that can neither be helped by better breathing
techniques nor by bringing on an attack.

172

High blood pressure (Oliehoek, 1981). The blood pressure group Utrecht-Overvecht shows an interesting combination of the use of self-help techniques with a self-help group approach. This combination has already been successfully tried in Zagreb. There are two parts to the meetings of these small groups. In the first part, both blood pressure and weight are recorded. This enables the noting of developments and changes, and individuals can find out which factors are influences on blood pressure.

In the second part, the influences on blood pressure are discussed. The information for such discussion is collected by the members themselves. So the members talk to each other about their ways of life and try to find the connection between factors causing high blood pressure and the blood pressure of each member of the group. Attention is given to such matters as:
- the use of cooking salt;
- the use of many ready-made products with a high sodium salt content;
- attitudes to stimulants such as alcohol, coffee and tobacco;
- the habits of an affluent society such as the eating of liquorice, salty biscuits, peppermints and other kinds of titbits;
- the consumption of 'wrong' foods, in the sense of too much animal protein and fat, hard fats and sugar;
- living in a society based on an economy that stimulates consumption;
- nervous tension, conflict and stress situations.

The results of this self-help group are very encouraging. An increasing sense of one's own responsibility and one's own capacity to work actively at one's own health has begun to develop. The investigations made indicated that the blood pressure of 40 per cent of the participants fell to a normal level. Moreover, it seems that it is not so much the techniques used that are responsible for these splendid results (e.g. saltless food or food rich in potassium), but the fact that people have begun to search for a more appropriate attitude to life.

A few reflections

Self-help as a new value in helping is a starting point for the fundamental reconstruction of health care. Such reconstruction will have to take place gradually. It is important that professional health staff such as GPs, nurses and pyschotherapists should be positively attuned to this development.

There are a number of implications in aiming at a health care system based on self-help. In the first place, the moth-eaten organisational thinking of our present pattern of health care needs to be altered. Policy-makers will have to abandon the view that the planning of facilities matters above all else, and realise that recovery in the community is the issue at stake. Much more attention will have to be given to informal forms of helping, to alternatives to the present health care system, and to the harmful side-effects of a bureaucratised system of health care. This is well illustrated by thinking in terms of echelons. In traditional thinking, there are three echelons of health care. The first echelon, that of primary health care carried out by GPs, district nurses, physiotherapists, and so on, acts as a reception area with a wide spectrum of facilities. The second echelon provides specialist and super specialist facilities. And the third echelon, that of nursing homes, and so on, is one in which the medical aspect recedes into the background.

This traditional thinking in terms of echelons needs to be extended by the development of an echelon between the individual and the primary health, as shown in Figure 1 below.

Figure 1   Echelons of Health Care

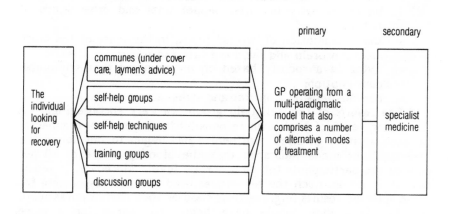

In addition, it will no longer be possible to ignore such substantial matters as how people recover, self-help techniques and so on, on account of the rise of alternative methods of treatment (Van Dijck, 1979; Nijs, 1979) and of the self-help movement. A greater multiplicity of cures, with more of them available in primary health care, is likely to result from this.

In primary health care, a much greater appeal will have to be made to the individual's own sense of responsibility. Several forms of voluntary work, training and discussion groups, self-help groups, and so on, ought to be stimulated. It is encouraging to see what is already happening by way of initiatives in the field of primary health care in the Netherlands (Geelen et al, 1980; de Jongh, 1980; van Dijk, 1978). These initiatives should be taken up by the population and by health workers in order that health care may gain a stronger collective dimension and become more firmly rooted in the population as a whole.

The developments that have been discussed here are mostly recent ones. It is clear that fresh possibilities will have to be explored. To this end, the Tilburg Self-help Project has drawn up a middle- to long-range research programme. We are glad to say that the request to work out such a programme originated from the Director-General of Public Health. It cannot be said that government policy in the Netherlands (cf. also Van Loon, 1981) has ignored developments towards a new pattern of health care.

Note
This is a shortened version of an article originally written as an introduction to a loose-leaf reference work entitled Zelfhulptechnieken (Self-help techniques) published in 1981 by Van Loghum Slaterus.

References
Bandler, R. and Grinder, J. (1981) Frogs into Princes, Real People Press, Moab, Letah.
Compernolle, T. (1981) 'De zelfbehandeling van recidiverende angstaanvallen en andere hyperventilatieverschijnselen' (Self-treatment of attacks of terror and other hyperventilation experiences) in R. Lafaille et al (eds), Zelfhulptechnieken: Wat het individu zelf kan doen aan zijn lichamelijk en geestelijk welzijn (Self-help techniques: what the individual can do himself about his own physical and psychical welfare), loose-leaf edition, Van Loghum Slaterus, Deventer.
Dijk, P. van (1978) Naar een gezonde gezondheidszorg (To a healthy health care), Ankh-Hermes, Deventer.
Dijk, P. van (1979) Geneeswijzen in Nederland: Compendium voor de niet-universitaire geneeskunde (Modes of treatment in the Netherlands: compendium for non-academic medicine), Ankh-Hermes, Deventer.
Geelen, K., Lafaille, R., Tilborghs, D.J. and Wegman, M. (1981) Initiatieven tot eigen verantwoordelijkheid in de gezondheidszorg (Initiatives in self-care and individual responsibility for health in the Netherlands), IVG, Tilburg.
Harberden, P. van and Lafaille, R. (eds) (1979a) Zelfhulp, een nieuwe vorm van hulpverlening? (Self-help: a new form of helping?), Vuga, 's-Gravenhage.
Harberden, P. van and Lafaille, R. (1979b), 'Over zelfhulpgroepen en professionals', (On self-help groups and professionals), Anders, 2, 8-17.

Jongh, T.O.M. de (1980) 'Werken met patienten: Ervaringen met een patientenraad' (Working with patients: experiences with a patients' council), <u>Huisarts en Wetenschap</u> (GP and Science), vol.23, 383-386.

Lafaille, R. et al (eds) (1981) <u>Zelfhulptechnieken: Wat het individu zelf kan doen aan zijn lichamelijk en geestelijk welzijn</u> (Self-help techniques: what the individual can do himself about his own physical and psychic welfare), loose-leaf edition, Van Loghum Slaterus, Deventer.

Loon, P.C.J. van (1981) 'Eigen verantwoordelijkheid voor gezondheid: objekt van overheidsbeleid in 1980' (Individual responsibility for heatlh: object of government policy in 1980) in R. Lafaille et al, <u>op.cit.</u>.

Nijs, P(ed) (1979), Alternative geneeswijzen (Alternative modes of treatment), special edition of <u>Farmaceutisch Tijdschrift roor Belgie</u> Vol. 56, 6.

Oliehoek, J. (1981) 'Zelfhulp bij hoge bloeddruk' (Self-help with high blood pressure), in R. Lafaille et al, <u>op.cit.</u>.

Roszak, T. (1975) <u>Unfinished Animal, the Aquarian Frontier and the Evolution of Consciousness</u>, Harper and Row, New York.

SUPPORT FOR SELF-HELP
Bert Bakker and Mathieu Karel

Introduction
Developments in self-help come from within as motive or
incentive, but can also be achieved by removing obstacles or by
creating a favourable environment. It is the environment of
self-help groups with which this article is concerned.

The decision to participate in a group entails a number of
changes for the individual in his/her social relationships. Becoming
a member is a change in itself, but there is also change as far as
others are concerned, such as relatives and friends. The degree of
approval and understanding of these others exerts an influence on
the participation of the individual. The individual deciding to
participate not only has to cope with a change in relationships with
friends and relatives but with a change in the definition of these
relationships as well. Many self-help groups take this into
consideration. Groups of handicapped people promote the
involvement of relatives by means of social evenings; while
multiple sclerosis groups encourage patients to work, together with
their partners and relatives, towards a better way of life and of
coping, and so on. Thus from the point of view of the individual,
the relatives form the primary environment to which attention
should be given, and from which opportunities for development may
arise.

Looked at from the point of view of the group, opportunities
for development are plentiful. For instance, there are different
buildings which are used during the day by institutions concerned
with health care, social work or education, which are empty in the
evening. These can be used by groups provided that they obtain
permission of the professionals in charge. This simple example
points to the most important element in the environment of
self-help groups: professionals in welfare, social work and health
care.

What we are concerned with is self-help defined as
'improvement activities of companions in distress'. We shall not
dicuss individual self-help methods. Our evidence comes from our
research in the Netherlands: partly from a survey (Bakker and
Karel, 1980) and partly from suggestions for improvements arising
out of particular local situations, as well as from numerous
discussions with group members. We also draw on information
from other countries. We begin with a general inventory of the

177

possibilities for supporting self-help, and finish with the policy implications.

Analysis of possibilities for support

In order to present in an orderly way the possibilities for support which can be found in the self-help environment, we shall use the following matrix. We first distinguish between:

1. Direct and material forms of support, among which we consider donations and government grants;
2. Indirect and material support, for example, money for research. A lateral effect of this activity is to draw more attention to self-help. We include in this second form of support the re-training of professionals and health education and promotion;
3. Direct and non-material systems, among which can be considered training by professionals for self-help groups, as well as research; and
4. Indirect and non-material assistance which includes general public education.

Material support can be offered in the form of finance (direct) as well as in the form of facilities (indirect). Non-material support can be given as services (by acting directly or by working on the surroundings) and in the form of guidelines. This framework provides a basis for discussing the multiplicity of measures which can be taken to affect the environment of self-help.

Direct and material

In the surroundings of self-help groups there are often professionals and professional organisations functioning as go-betweens or intermediaries in obtaining the necessary financial support. The organisations play the role of an umbrella protecting the group from the authority granting the subsidy and guaranteeing that the money will serve a good purpose. This go-between function can be expanded without too much difficulty. In this way professional organisations and their employees provide for the needs of organised groups which have no access of their own to financial resources.

In the context of the current criticism of health care and welfare work the strengthening of this facilitative role would be welcome. In this way professional organisations can form an umbrella for self-help groups which cannot by themselves meet the official conditions for the receiving of grants. In the Netherlands, the Koningin Juliana Fonds (K.J.F.) has since 1979 distributed yearly about one million Dutch guilders to self-help groups. Other private foundations also provide money for such organsiations.

In addition, in the field of voluntary work in the Netherlands, there are a number of service organisations which are able to provide direct material support. Both the National Voluntary

Activities Centre (ELVAS) and the National Workshop Foundation (Landelijke Stichting Werkwinkel) offer support to voluntary organisations. ELVAS in Amsterdam has, for instance, a printing press at its disposal which can be used by self-help and other groups. The Centre also offers non-material support such as training and information as well as administrative assistance. Werkwinkel in Utrecht offers information about voluntary work and advice and assistance to those involved in it. For instance, it has special arrangements for supporting bereavement groups. The Stichting Gezondheidsvoorlichting (Werkgroep 2000) in Amersfoort offers support in the field of health care and publishes a national patients' newspaper.

In this article, the possibilities for financial support from municipal authorities will not be discussed, despite the fact that the planned decentralisation of social welfare in the Netherlands is likely to make these of increasing importance. However, the possibilities for support at the local level are numerous. Groups can usually obtain such material support as meeting rooms and duplicating facilities from many social service and religious institutions. Moreover, there are volunteer bureaux in the Netherlands where people who are willing to do something for others can register. Self-help groups can make use of these human resources. There are also telephone S.O.S. services run by volunteers which can act in support of self-help groups. These services often have good 'social maps' of the local situation. There are many more such support possibilities abroad as can be seen from the work of such commentators as: Hollstein and Perth (1980) for Germany, Austria and Switzerland, Young and Rigge (1980) for England and Lieberman and Borman (1979) and Gartner and Riessman (1980) for America.

Above an attempt was made to summarise a number or mediating functions, in particular the one of acting as an intermediary between grant-giving agencies and self-help groups, where the absence of government financial arrangements makes this necessary. These functions can, however, be extended along the lines of the American 'clearing-houses', which combine various forms of support. In the Dutch context this suggestion would mean even more welfare organisations and umbrella bodies linking them together.

Indirect and material

Government recognition of the importance of these mediating functions would mean indirect as well as direct support for self-help groups. They need people for secretarial work. Often volunteers act as substitutes in fulfilling this task, but there is a demand for paid professional work as well. Indirect material support could be given by explicitly devoting time to self-help groups within traditional courses for social work and for health professionals. Thus students would be better prepared to act in a supportive role.

Within the framework of the health service, the statutory authorities can offer material support to many private associations within a particular category. In the Netherlands, for instance, there is the M.S. Foundation for multiple sclerosis patients. It publishes its own bulletin and is in contact with specialist clinics. Within the foundation self-help groups are flourishing. Help from this kind of foundation brings patients into contact with each other. In following a policy of this kind the government will have to shift its orientation from the individual to categories and groups. However, such a shift in government policy can take place without much damage being done to existing groups. It can also generate useful support for many associations of patients as well as for individual members.

Indirect material help can also be given in the form of subsidies for applied or action research. Thus, applied or action research can be used and, through a trial and error method, new possibilities can be tried out with those involved (see Pinker, 1971; de Vries, 1977, and so on). In other countries there are even more facilities for self-help groups at national, regional and local level. These various clearing-houses and self-help centres offer scope for combining different kinds of support in a variety of ways.

Direct and non-material

This kind of support involves education for groups and also for individuals from the public at large. Many weekly publications and women's magazines nowadays give attention to self-help. They provide information, supply addresses and relate real-life stories. These could be the basis for a documentation centre which would make available this and other kinds of information for groups and individuals. Such a centre would only store information and would offer no other kind of support. The Ministry of Health in the Netherlands intends to set up such a centre. Another, perhaps more obvious, possibility is to expand further the existing organisations concerned with voluntary work. This would mean more co-operation between organisations to establish a stronger infrastructure.

ELVAS, Werkwinkel and Stichting 2000 have already been mentioned. In conjunction with local voluntary centres, these can be seen as a network within which co-operation to support self-help groups can be stimulated. As stated above, these groups can provide direct support, but there is also a lot they can do by way of public education and enlightenment. These voluntary organisations have a dual function; they give information about self-help to people having difficulties; and at the same time they recruit volunteers who want to do something for other people. Another important information network is that formed by the 22 MAIC offices (Social Advice and Information Centres) scattered all over the country. All relevant information about self-help groups is available from them. The local centres collect their own information and also receive new information from the national centre.

In America researchers have been particularly active in supplying information about self-help groups in the form of directories. They spend a great deal of time tracking down and making inventories of them, in order to obtain more data for their research. The same useful role has also been played by researchers in Belgium and Germany (Brankaerts, 1980; Moeller, 1981). In the Netherlands, van Harberden and Lafaille have, among other researchers, gathered information about a number of groups which has been published in the form of inventories (Jansen et al, 1979).

Professionals in welfare work and health care form another segment in the environment of self-help groups. Gartner and Riessman (1980), for instance, have distinguished the following possibilities for support from these groups - professionals can refer, can help groups to develop themselves and can do staff jobs. Some professionals are experienced in practice-oriented research, planning programmes or even in campaigning. Self-help groups can use these capabilities (Caplan, 1974; Silverman, 1976, 1980; Bakker and Karel, 1979). There is a highly developed infrastructure of professionals in the Netherlands and many groups want to be recognised in this sector.

Important direct and non-material support can be given through legislation and the law. Groups may benefit from clearly defined and delimited rights for patients. Rights to free assembly, to information and to privacy should be granted to self-help groups as well as to individual citizens.

Indirect and non-material

This kind of support concerns the creation of a favourable context for self-help groups. More attention could be given to self-help in health education in schools and when giving guidance and information to the public. In the training of professionals more time could be devoted to self-help and government ministers could provide stimulation through the right kind of pronouncements. These are forms of indirect support which cost no money but which create a better working climate.

A considerable amount of development has taken place in America which is relevant to the present discussion. Since the closure of the HUD (Department of Housing and Urban Development) and the increasing effects of the Reagan administration, large numbers of support structures by way of research centres and programmes have come to an end. There is little prospect of policy developments favouring self-help during the Reagan administration. Policy means spending, and policy towards self-help groups is no exception.

However, in the past commissions were appointed and suggestions have been made. Lieberman and Borman (1979) quote a numer of recommendations made by the President's Commission on Mental Health concerning self-help. The following initiatives are mentioned there:

- the recongition and strengthening of naturally helping networks such as self-help groups;
- the consolidation of social support functions of the existing official care institutions;
- the improvement of inter-communication between formal (official) and natural networks;
- the development of strategies with regard to the public and professionals, concerning the nature and the function of self-help and natural helping networks, as well as the importance of solidarity and reciprocity for welfare;
- the initiation of research to gather up to date information about such networks, to ascertain the direction and the amplitude of changes in them, as well as to enhance knowledge about how they achieve their aims.

These recommendations are also relevant in the European context.

The policy of the Dutch government

There is no actual government policy concerning self-help organisations. The accent lies mainly on individual care, performed by individuals (Hattinga Verschure, 1977). Thus two approaches are relevant: one on voluntary policy and one on health care. Both are tricky subjects. When cuts in expenditure are being implemented, the giving of more attention to voluntary work may appear dubious. In addition, new social developments are taking place which cast a fresh light on the role of volunteers. By this we mean the women's movement and discussions about home care, fostering, the right to paid work, inequalities of pay and threats to existing jobs.

In the appendix to its preliminary report, the inter-departmental commission on Policy for Volunteers considers, among other things, the opinions of the officials of the Ministry of Health:

One of the most essential tasks of the health care organisations and authorities for the future is the promotion of an increased capacity on the part of citizens to manage by themselves and the reduction of the dependence of the potential consumer on the professional system.

In a covering letter from the Minister of CRM (Culture, Recreation and Social Work) one can read the following:

The government is of the opinion that it should be part of the code of professionals to co-operate with and give assistance to volunteers and self-help groups. At the same time steps will be taken to ensure that a place will be found in the process of training and educating professionals for the acquisition of knowlege and skills enabling them to deal better with volunteers.

In an earlier phase Mr. Hendriks, then Secretary for Health, declared that the population should be less dependent and take its own decisions for the furtherance of health. This points towards self-help, voluntary work and decentralisation. In a commentary on the budget of the Ministry of Health for 1979 it was written that the citizen not only has rights but also obligations with regard to his/her own health.

For the time being, the main factor in policy concerning self-help seems to be the Ministry of Health. There is no doubt about the good intentions in these pronouncements, but up to now there are barely any guidelines to indicate the way these intentions will be brought into effect. This tends to create the impression that the government is trying to disclaim responsibility. The emphasis laid on the role of the individual can imply that the citizen is going to be deprived of something without getting anything back in exchange.

It seems as though government will seek to use self-help as a technique forming part of first-line health care. This would make the possibility of the consumer exercising an influence as remote as it was in the past. Hence it is in the interests of self-help groups to form independent, separate entities parallel to the official infrastructure.

With regard to this, it is worth noting the developments concerning the democratisation of social work, with reference to the report of the Van der Burg Commission. These are not very encouraging since they leave the position of professionals almost intact, not recognising the rejection by self-help groups of their patronising attitudes.

The Provincial Cultural Councils are also giving more attention to the subject of self-help. In this case there is a danger of professionals taking over the methods and models developed by the groups themselves. Thus the VOS courses (Women and Society) originally organised by housewives are now being run by the Cultural Councils as part of their adult education work.

Decentralisation is likely to increase the role of local authorities. The Rijksbijdrageregeling Sociaal Cultureel Werk (the Arrangement for Governmental Assistance to Social and Cultural Work), for example, creates the possibility for support for local groups on a local basis. This will make the ideological colour of local municipalities more significant. For example, will councils with a strongly religious orientation support feminist activities?

Tensions exist in the relationships between self-help and the authorities. For example, authorities like to draw up inventories and put groups into categories compatible with existing organisational arrangements, thus facilitating control over them.

Self-help groups, on the other hand, want recognition from the institutions and the professionals, but on the basis of equality. This indicates the kind of contact institutions usually have with each other.

Help only where it helps: a pragmatic point of view

Self-help means different things to different people. A participant in a self-help group is likely to ascribe a different sense to the word as compared with a policy-maker concerned with improving the health behaviour of the public through self-help. The tendency is to develop a policy for self-help within the institutions of the health and welfare world. If policy for self-help is made predominantly within this context we fear that the idea of self-help may be deformed.

A different sort of policy is required for self-help. The essence of it should be an educative attitude on the part of the authorities, following developments at grass roots and consulting with those concerned. In this way initiatives would be allowed much more space. This would involve only a modest scale of intervention from government. As we see it, self-help groups should not be classified under existing structures. Separate provision should be made with separate policy-making.

Regarding the implementation of policy, of great importance would be the creation of a separate organisation, able to embark on honest consultations with the groups and those involved with them. In this way a complementary policy could be developed out of the exchange of experience between groups. In fact, what we are talking about is a policy for stimulation and development which would be applied across different policy areas. The instrument of this policy would be an agency which would have the trust of the groups and would maintain regular contact with them. Its agenda would be developed from our matrix of the different kinds of support needed by groups.

References and relevant literature

Bakker, B. and Karel, M. (1980) 'Self-help groups and mutual aid in the Netherlands: survey research' (paper presented at 1st World Congress of IVAR/Voir, Brussels, June 1980) in B. Bakker, M. Karel and I. Sewandono, Vehicles in Welfare Achievement: self-help, self-care and public care. Three working papers, IWA Voorpublicatie, University of Amsterdam.

Bakker, B. and Karel, M. (eds.) (1979) Zelfhulp en Welzijnswerk: Ervaringen van profesionals met zelfgeleide groepen, Samson, Alphen aan den Rijn.

Branckaerts, J. (1980) Voorlopige Inventaris van Zelfulpgroepen in Vlaanderen, Soc. Onderzoeksinstituut, Kath. Universiteit, Leuven.

Caplan, G. (1974) Support Systems and Community Mental Health: Lectures on concept development, Behavioural Publications, New York.

Gartner, A. and Riessman, F. (1980) Help: a working guide to self-help groups, New Viewpoints/Vision, Franklin Watts, New York.

Hattinga Verschure, J. (1977) Het Berschijnsel Zorg, De Tijdstroom, Lochem.

Hollstein, W. and Perth, B. (1980) Alternative Projekte: Beispielem gegen die resignation, Rowolht, Reinbek bei Hamburg.

Jansen, H., Lafaille, R., van Harberden, P. and Postma, L. (1979) Zelfhulpgroepen in Nederland (5 vols), Projektgroep zelfhulp, Kath. Hogeschool Tilburg.

Lieberman, M. and Borman, L. et. al., (1979) Self-help Groups for Coping with Crisis, Jossey Bass, San Fransisco.

Mellet, J. (1980) 'Self-help, mental health and professionals' in S. Hatch (ed.), Mutual Aid and Social and Health Care, ARVAC/Bedford Square Press, London.

Moeller, M. (1981) Anders Helfen: selbsthilfegruppen und fachleute arbeiten zusammen, Klett, Stuttgart.

Pinker, R. (1971) Social Theory and Social Policy, Heinemann, London.

Silverman, P. (1976) 'The widow as care giver in a programme of preventive intervention with other widows', in G. Caplan and M. Killilea (eds), Support Systems and Mutual Help: Multidisciplinary explorations, Grune and Stratton, New York.

Silverman, P. (1980) Mutual Self-help Groups: organisation and development, Sage, California.

Vries, T. de (1977) Self-help Groepen: een verkenning naar de funktie en werking van self-help groepen, Lorp, NVAGG, Utrecht.

Young, M. and Rigge, M. (1979) Mutual Aid in a Selfish Society: a plea for strengthening the co-operative movement, Mutual Aid Press, London.

MUTUAL AID: FROM RESEARCH TO SUPPORTIVE POLICY - REPORT FROM A WHO WORKSHOP

This workshop was a joint venture of the German Federal Ministry of Youth, Family Affairs and Health, the Federal Centre for Health Education, the WHO Information Centre on Research into Self-Help and Health (part of the Hamburg Project Gesundheitsselbsthilfegruppen), the Division for Medical Sociology of the K.U. Leuven and WHO Regional Office for Europe, Health Education Department. Twenty-five people from seven countries took part. It was held at Hohr-Grenzhausen in June 1982. What follows is an edited version of the concluding part of the report on the workshop written by Jan Branckaerts and Christiane Deneke.

Constraints and Enabling Factors

It is important to be aware of enabling factors and constraints that affect the development of self-help. These can operate at different levels.

(a) <u>At the level of institutions and organisations</u>. Some of the most recalcitrant problems are found at this level. To begin with, most existing bureaucracies and hierarchies are at the opposite end of the organisational spectrum from the spontaneous and informal structures that often characterise self-help groups: hence a possible lack of official or institutional understanding and exclusion from power and influence in favour of established professionals. At the same time there is the risk that self-help group autonomy and creativity will be threatened by the involvement of the state and other authorities, and the danger that self-help group development might be distorted by crude efficiency concepts. One of the main dangers may be the restriction of self-help group development due to excessively narrow definitions of health or of self-help groups that might be imposed by conventional bureaucracies. This could perhaps arise where existing bureaucracies view the tasks of self-help groups from an approach that emphasises medically defined disease or ill health.

(b) <u>At the political and cultural level</u>. Current official and political attitudes do not in general favour a wider range of responsibilities for self-help groups. Support of collective self-help is not yet included in the legislation and regulations of welfare systems, even when the primary health care approach has been adopted.   In principle, governments may regard self-help essentially as cheap health care and thus have a distorted approach

186

to it; there is, of course, the possibility that political or statutory support may undermine the autonomy of self-help groups in unacceptable ways.

(c) At the professional level. Clearly, relations between the professions and self-care are bound to be of critical importance. Quite serious and unnecessary limitations can be imposed on self-help groups by ostensibly supportive professional organisations which, in fact, dictate the type of support they give and which often have vested interests in what groups achieve. In general, of course, there is an in-built orientation of welfare systems towards professional services. Where professionals do develop relations with self-help groups, a recurrent problem is that their involvement is often too early or precipitate and too close, and may well inhibit the movement towards collective self-help.

(d) At the research level. In spite of the emphasis on the autonomy of self-help groups, especially with regard to their goals, researchers may still approach with preconceived ideas of the particular tasks of self-help groups. In general, of course, current research priorities are mostly concerned with technical and somatic medicine and, as such, hinder the development of social science and epidemiological research on the lay system and an understanding of a social concept of health.

Given these constraints, it is apparent that those subject to various forms of external authority, whether professional or otherwise, will develop a corresponding lack of confidence in their own ability to help others or themselves. Together with a widespread lack of awareness of self-help group opportunities, this negative view clearly hinders the development of self-help groups.

As far as self-help groups themselves are concerned, there are the difficulties involved in creating new forms of organisation due to a lack of experience or confidence. In terms of collective support systems, there may be problems in developing joint interests when individual group interests may be disparate and time and resources limited.

Obviously, if governments and people in general accepted the broad WHO definition of health, the basis for the development of self-help groups would be much more secure. Likewise, a move away from cure and towards care would facilitate general support for self-help. The greater public visibility of successful self-help groups and their support systems would help to transform the political and cultural climate in their favour. Self-help groups and their support systems promote community participation in the health service system and can thus promote a consumer-centred health policy. Finally, it is vital to take account of the variations in local and national circumstances and accordingly to adopt a flexible approach to particular models.

The development of concepts and practices of self-help, as techniques that lay people can use, help to overcome the constraints experienced by individuals. The importance of a suitable climate of opinion to help people overcome problems of authority orientation is fundamental, helping to shift attention from producers to consumers and helping people to take a more positive view of their own abilities as helpers. To create such a climate there must be a multiplication of successful autonomous self-help groups and support systems.

Guiding principles for support systems

Two principles should guide the development and functioning of support centres: these are flexibility and non-directiveness. Flexibility refers to the fact that the model should vary according to the particular local and national conditions. Thus the functions should be adapted so as to take into account the existing groups and their needs, the health and welfare system of the area or country and the economic, social and political structure as well as the cultural elements shaping the society and the state.

Non-directiveness refers to the fact that a principal aim of support centres is to facilitate self-help groups to achieve the goals they choose. Since a support centre should help to make possible what self-help groups and organisations want to do and should in no way determine self-help group actions and strategies, support centres cannot be responsible for these actions. The kind of support should not be dictated by the support centre and the achievements of self-help groups should not be claimed as those of the support centre.

The word 'professional' - so easily used - has in this context at least two different meanings: it is used to refer to medical-technical experts in the problems dealt with by the various groups, as well as to experts in self-help group processes or in psychosocial aspects of health. Groups might want to take into account the expertise of both of them, one of them or neither of them - according to their own self-help group policy. The support centre, however, should create access to the expertise of both of them if asked to.

Although the workshop mainly concentrated on territorially defined general support systems, it in no way excluded the development of specialist support systems. This refers to the banding together of different self-help organisations or self-help groups dealing with the same problem or a category of related problems. This can be an effective way of supporting the achievement of self-help organisations' goals. But the workshop was of the opinion that these category specific alliances should primarily be initiated by the groups and organisations themselves and that support centres should play an instrumental role in bringing them into existence.

Functions of a Support Centre

The functions of a support centre were identified as information and documentation, provision of resources, facilitation and outreach and innovation. Without being exhaustive or exclusive, the following concrete examples were given.

<u>Information and Documentation</u>. This includes collecting addresses of self-help groups and organisations; maintaining an up-to-date databank; providing information or referral to those who call upon the centre. Documentation comprises the gathering of all kinds of material pertaining to the groups as well as to the problems they deal with. The popularisation of scientific research data and the facilitation of research and assistance in the development of self-help research might also be seen as functions of a support centre. The publication of regular newsletters, papers and reports might help the execution of these functions.

<u>The provision of material resources</u> was considered to be of the utmost importance: this means making available such resources as rooms, printing, reprographic and general office equipment, together with instruction in the use of such facilities.

<u>Facilitation and Outreach</u>. Under this heading the support centre function rests on a positive evaluation of self-help. It includes encouragement, support and the conduct of training activities for specific self-help groups and their organisations; facilitating collaboration with professionals and the delineation of territories; provision of expertise relevant to the training of professionals about self-help, ways to deal with active patients and on how to work with mutual aid groups. It can also include policy analysis for specific self-help organisations or in a more general way for self-help as a whole; addressing and influencing professional and public policy audiences as to the activities of self-help groups, their relationship with professional providers and their relevance to public policy issues; the influencing of public opinion in favour of patients active in their own treatment and in favour of self-help groups; finally it includes assistance to the media in presenting realistic pictures of self-help groups and in correcting distorted images.

Under an additional heading 'innovation' those functions and activities could be listed that pertain to the development of new models, new strategies or new processes in the field of self-help groups.

Levels of operation

Some comments were made about support centres operating on different levels: local, national and international.

On the local level the workshop generally agreed that the emphasis should be on providing material resources, technical support, information and documentation on self-help groups and other relevant resources like professional resources or the community resource centres, etc., serving as a bridge and buffer between lay and professional support systems.

The local support centre should use existing informal networks as much as possible and should adopt a low key approach especially in the beginning, trying to respond to needs expressed by existing and nascent self-help groups. While in large urban areas this can be done through a support centre, in smaller urban areas and in most rural areas it might be necessary to allocate the resource and support functions to centres already existing in the community or to a new centre that, besides self-help groups, would also serve other community based groups and organisations.

On the national level, the workshop observed that many national governments and other non-governmental funding bodies are already supporting specific national organisations so that they can support their local groups. Sometimes this special support is selective in favouring the older well-established self-help organisations. The workshop took the view that younger, newer self-help organisations should get equal access to resources and that in general the development of a national support system should not interfere with the assistance given to organisations and groups.

The national support centre should concentrate on the self-help organisations and on the coordination and support given to local support centres. Here the provision of material resources might be less important. It was thought of rather as an interfacing structure that would facilitate contacts between self-help organisations, the professional world, the research community, the government and the general public, by making visible what the groups are doing and making knowledge about developments available to the parties concerned.

On the international level the development of information centres such as the one at Hamburg is vital. By means of networking, information exchange, the organisation of conferences and the publication of reports, an international centre could collect and disseminate information and provide coordination and support to a multiplicity of users. It could do so for national research in self-help as well as for national support centres, and finally it could coordinate and support international self-help organisations and enable them to represent their constituency at conferences of medical specialists dealing with topics with which the self-help organisation is concerned, thus establishing a structure for consumer participation.

The interaction and collaboration between all these levels can be seen as follows. The local levels should sustain and suport the local groups; the national levels the national organisations that work for the local groups; the international level the international self-help organisations. In addition the international level should sustain and support the national levels and the national levels the regional and local levels. In this way a general support system could sustain the specialist support system of its own level, and the generalist support system on lower levels.

On the basis of its discussions, the workshop put forward the following recommendations to WHO. These were endorsed by another WHO workshop held at Hohr-Grenzhausen in February 1983 on Mutual Aid and Professional Care.

WHO is recommended:
- to continue facilitating the exchange of experience about collective self-help and relevant support systems on all levels;
- to support responsive and supportive research into self-help in health and the lay system in general, putting special emphasis on support structures;
- to press for changes in relevant professional training both internationally (for instance in international training courses for health education workers) and nationally, to enable professionals to develop knowledge and understanding of self-help groups and their role in health care:
- to ensure the continuity and appropriate growth of the 'Information Centre on Research into Self-Health', so it can meet the growing needs for networking, especially as more national support centres come into existence;
- to sponsor and support resource oriented support centres with special emphasis on health matters, based on the needs of self-help groups. This implies the initiation of support centres, preferably by the encouragement of appropriate existing initiatives to take up this function. Comparative evaluation should be made available.

WHO is recommended to urge national governments:
- to develop national policies supporting self-help in line with the recommendations and in the light of the proceedings of this workshop;
- to facilitate the work of existing and the initiation of new national support centres and to establish a timetable for this by the end of 1984 (7th Program of Work), and to support the development of lay health care as a programme of WHO;
- to urge local and regional authorities to facilitate the work of existing and the initiation of new local self-help groups;
- to ensure representation of self-help groups and organisations directly or via support systems at all relevant levels in decision-making bodies as one way of ensuring consumer participation in the health care system.

MAKING A PLACE FOR SELF-HELP
Stephen Hatch and Ilona Kickbusch

The contributions to this book bear witness to a growing body of opinion that supports an active role for lay people in health. They show how in all sorts of ways and from all sorts of starting points both lay people and professionals are taking initiatives aimed at putting more responsibility for their own health into the hands of people whose qualification is that they know about a problem from their own experience. The main, but not the only vehicle for doing this, is the self-help group - a voluntary and usually informal expression of collective action. The groups themselves are very diverse, but a number of general points arise from their activities and these are reflected in the contributions to this book.

The role of self-help
As stated in the introduction, at a practical level groups are vehicles for sharing experiences, passing on useful knowledge and offering and receiving emotional and moral support. They have flourished particularly amongst those with chronic conditions or handicaps, among people experiencing life crises or with psychiatric problems and among those with a disadvantaged social status. They deal mainly with problems medicine cannot cure; mainly they are concerned with coping and prevention rather than alternative ways of curing; and the core of their method is to provide for their members an alternative or deliberately created community.

At a more ideological level self-help serves to influence how problems and issues are defined. Putting it in a basic and elementary way, the problems faced by the sufferer or group member are personal ones; they cannot be defined only in medical terms or only in social terms; they do not fall exclusively within the domain of any particular medical or social profession or any particular institution through with the professions provide their services. By coming together group members are able to establish alternative definitions of their condition and reinforce these through mutual support. This ideological/practical tension is often presented, as it has been by Trojan, as a dichotomy between changing the individual and changing the system. Reality seems more complicated than this and has more of a dialectic character. Both sorts of change often go together and contribute to each other. Recognising the limits of medicine is an incentive both to

192

the assumption by lay people of greater skills and competence and to the formulation of different expectations of the health care system.

For this reason mutual aid groups attract professionals who want to change the ways in which medical and social problems are defined and responded to. This explains the interest in this field of most of the physicians and social scientists who have contributed to this book. Recognising the limitations of existing intellectual and institutional structures, they see in self-help groups a lever for change and a way of taking health care out of the consulting room or the operating theatre into the community.

It is not always clear whether this movement into the community is an expression of colonialism or of subversion, of professionals seeking to exert a more pervasive if more subtle influence on the behaviour of the lay population, or of lay people challenging the assumptions and prerogatives of the medical professions. Movement in both directions seems to be in progress.

Thus self-help is two things. Partly it is the practical and emotional support offered to each other by members of self-help groups. But it is also an arena where, unbeknown to many of the group members, fundamental issues of medicine and health and of the responsibilities of health care systems are being contested.

The ideological and political debate will not be settled in these pages, nor should or will the development of self-help wait upon the definitive resolution of ideological questions. But before returning to a discussion of more pragmatic and practical measures, one further point should be made which may help to move forward debate about the role of mutual aid groups.

In recent years self-help has flourished both in the USA and in Britain, that is both under a free enterprise health system and under a centralised national health service, as well as in European countries with systems that lie somewhere between these two poles. Today, advocacy of self-help is to be heard both on the right and on the left of the political spectrum. Thus self-help cuts across many traditional political and structural differences. Populist it certainly is, but it is a kind of populism that calls for fresh thinking and fresh political and social alignments, not stock responses from established positions. This is because mutual aid suggests changes in the roles of lay people, professionals and the state, not just movements in the boundary between the responsibilities of the state and the private person.

This may be one of the reasons why the response of governments and health authorities has so far not been clear cut and decisive. Most commentators have been prepared to applaud self-help in a general way, and few have attacked it. Nevertheless for the most part its role is still perceived as marginal to the health care system. The case made directly or indirectly by the contributions to this book is that mutual aid deserves support as a valuable complement to the health care system. As already argued this case is partly ideological, partly pragmatic. The ideological case has been and continues to be quite widely stated and is supported, as in this book, by examples of actual groups and self-help activities. The issues that have been less adequately dealt with are the more pragmatic ones. They fall under two headings - issues of efficacy and issues of distribution. In other words, what are the benefits of participation in self-help and who are the beneficiaries?

Benefits of participation

Both issues can be dealt with be saying that self-help is a voluntary activity. Anyone who wants to join or set up a self-help group can do so. Likewise only those who feel it benefits them will continue to take part. Thus the growth of self-help and the readiness of participants to say how it helps them are, it can be argued, evidence enough. After all, part of the message of self-help is that what is a problem, what is a cure or solution and what is an acceptable way of living with a problem are questions which people must answer for themselves, rather than taking for granted the judgements of the professionals.

These propositions may be a sufficient basis for suggesting to individuals that they try out self-help for themselves. However they do not provide strong grounds for a more widespread recognition of self-help and the allocation of publicly provided financial support. In any case the individual considering whether to join a group and the professional advising on this can reasonably ask for other evidence besides the testimony of participants.

Sympathetic commentators usually cite examples of good or successful groups. In practice not all groups do provide a good experience, certainly not for everyone. A number of specific claims are usually made for self-help. Generally these are about coping or living with problems or preventing them from getting worse, not about curing them. This means that much self-help is about subjective feelings and states of mind rather than physical functioning. Thus, as argued in the introduction, conventional medical criteria that relate to improvements in physical functioning are insufficient for judging the achievements of self-help groups. In many cases it will be more relevant to ask, for example, whether participants become more self confident, lose a sense of stigma, feel less lonely and isolated, have learnt better ways of coping, and so on. Such subjective changes in participants are susceptible to empirical assessment. It is also possible to study group processes and the way groups function, which would offer insights helpful to the practice of self-help. Yet relatively little work has been done on these social and psychological aspects. Among the contributors to this book only Grimsmo and his colleagues provide evidence of substance about outcomes, and this is on physical not psychological outcomes and relates to groups where self-help meant self-control. This dearth of evidence is partly because, in rejecting the medical model of health and the dominance of medical criteria, there has been a tendency to argue that the only evidence about self-help which has any meaning is of a purely phenomenological kind. In reality, as Branckaerts suggests in his discussion of research on self-help, these are not the only alternatives.

The proportion of the population at present involved in self-help groups cannot be calculated with any accuracy. Even if one confines oneself to relatively well defined conditions, for example having high blood pressure or a handicapped child or having had a mastectomy, it is difficult to relate the population in that situation to the number participating in relevant self-help groups. Nevertheless there can be little doubt that in all European countries actual participants as yet usually number only a small proportion of the potential participants. Tentative estimates of the proportion of the eligible population actually joining mutual aid groups suggests that one or two per cent is not unusual, though there are examples of much greater participation.

Some of the potential benefits from self-help are not confined to participants. For example, groups may stimulate improvements in the quality and the structure of institutional services and in the behaviour of professionals. But in so far as benefits are enjoyed only by participants, issues of distribution and equity arise. Thus situations are conceivable in which self-help groups, composed predominantly of the educated and articulate, capture a disproportionate share of professional attention and resources, perhaps even at the expense of less articulate people whose conditions are more severe. However, though some groups could develop in this direction, there is no evidence which confirms that this is what is happening. For the most part self-help groups constitute additional resources for health: they are not players in a zero sum game. Moreover, if they do have an effect on the distribution of publicly provided resources, it is likely to be a beneficial one in favour of chronic rather than acute conditions, since people with chronic conditions are more likely to join groups.

However this does not dispose of the issue of equity raised by the claim that self-help should be supported by public policy. Nor is it answered by asserting that because it is voluntary anyone who wants to can take part in mutual aid. If this was true it would be the answer, but in reality for a variety of reasons - economic, social, psychological and geographical - not everyone has the same capacity to initiate and sustain groups or an equal opportunity to take part in them. Furthermore, a single group cannot be expanded indefinitely without changing its nature and perhaps losing some of the qualities that make participation worthwhile. Hence if participation in self-help is to be extended, ways have to be found of forming new groups or sub-dividing existing ones. In theory this may not seem difficult, but in practice it does not always occur spontaneously, particularly if as sometimes happens a group is inclined to believe that in its locality there is not room for other groups concerned with the same problems. All this makes it pertinent to find out more about who does and who does not take part in self-help groups. It also indicates that in order to make self-help an option that is available to all appropriate forms of support are needed.

Supporting self-help

The argument can be illustrated very concretely. The members of a considerable number of self-help groups have limited mobility. Their condition may mean that they cannot afford private transport or that they cannot drive themselves. Consequently, unless transport is provided, participation may be limited to people who can rely on someone else to take them to meetings. Hence transport, both vehicles and their drivers, is a very necessary form of support. But given limited resources, at some point the choice has to be made between providing transport for existing group members (which is likely to be their first priority) and putting time and effort into involving new members and helping new groups to come into existence. Of course in practice it would usually be possible to attract extra help with transport and to strike a reasonable balance between services for existing members and efforts to involve new ones. Nevertheless two conclusions follow: there is a clear need for support and the basis upon which support is provided should ensure that not all the support is absorbed by existing participants.

The same argument can also be put in more general terms. Self-help is by definition something people do for themselves rather than have done to them by people who are paid. Nevertheless self-help can be expensive of the time of participants and, in particular, make large demands on some leading members of groups. It also takes a certain amount of confidence, some organisational skills and material resources like meeting rooms and transport to start groups and keep them going. The nature of some of the problems that are potentially the focus for self-help means that these resources can be in limited supply. Hence the case for making it easier to initiate and develop self-help groups by providing a limited amount of human and material support.

Hitherto, most of the support for self-help has come from sympathetic professionals, like those who have contributed to parts II and III of this book. They have developed a self-help dimension as part of their professional responsibilities. And to different degrees in different countries self-help has gained strength from broader movements for the reorientation of health care. In addition, there are now a number of projects or centres with the

196

specific purpose of supporting self-help. During the 1970's self-help groups spread rapidly in Europe. All sorts of innovations and spontaneous developments were taking place. But these have not yet brought self-help to the point where it is taken seriously by policy makers, or in medical education, or by the health professions generally. Nor is it yet widely accepted as an option that should be available to all. In these pages, as in many other reviews, the case for self-help has been strongly argued. What should the next steps be?

In essence what is needed in order to bring forth the next stage in the development of self-help is the creation of a supportive environment. Such an environment would offer active encouragement rather than simply passive tolerance. This calls for changes both inside and outside official health care systems.

Inside health care systems it is partly a matter of the attitudes of professionals, administrators and policy makers and of their willingness to recognise a self-help dimension in their work and so to respond helpfully to self-help groups. But the ability of health care institutions to respond helpfully is not just a matter of attitudes: it also requires an allocation of responsibilites such that there are identifiable individuals within the bureaucracies to whom self-help groups can turn.

However at the moment the majority of professionals are either not particularly interested in self-help or suspicious of it. This is one reason why some support for self-help should come from outside official health care systems. In addition part of the impetus behind self-help and of the rationale for it stems from the shortcomings and limitations of official professional systems; hence it will always be essential for self-help groups to be able to exist independently of official systems, even if the actual relationship between groups and the system is usually one of collaboration and partnership rather than conflict.

Only in the last few years has the need for some sort of support system for self-help begun to be recognised, and the development of actual arrangements for facilitating self-help is even more recent. Of course in many countries there have for a long time been national organisations which can be seen as federations of local self-help groups concerned with the same set of issues, from mental handicap to psoriasis. But as Judy Wilson points out in her contribution, the amount of help these national, specialist bodies can provide at the local level is often limited. In her account of the first year of the Nottingham Self-Help Groups Project she indicates that there is considerable scope for five support functions: helping new groups come into existence, helping existing groups with advice and facilities, bringing groups together to discuss matters of common interest, collecting and disseminating information about the groups that exist in the area and spreading knowledge and understanding about self-help among professionals. These correspond closely with the functions of local support centres identified by the WHO's Hohr-Grenzhausen workshop. The workshop also argued that equivalent functions ought to be carried out at national and international levels.

In Britain the Nottingham project is a unique pioneering venture. Elsewhere in Europe similar projects exist in Belgium (Leuven), Netherlands (Maastricht) and the Federal Republic of Germany (Hamburg). As stated in the contribution by Ellis Huber, a large self-help support project is being established in West Berlin in close cooperation with a major voluntary agency, the Deutsche Paritatische Wohlfahrtsverband.

At present no one is claiming that there is only one correct way of supporting self-help, or that there is only one model for a support system, saving only that support should be non-directive in character and respect the autonomy of the groups. What can be said with confidence is that over the next few years there is a great opportunity to develop a variety of arrangements for supporting self-help. With the aid of research that would identify the potentialities and test the achievements both of support centres and of self-help itself, these would constitute important steps towards a re-orientation of health care.

Here, therefore, is an agenda for the 1980's. Making a place for self-help does require material resources, but of a quantity that is infinitesimal in relation to the total health budget and infinitesimal in relation to budgets for the development of high technology medicine. Thus in terms of resources the agenda is a modest one, but it is ambitious in how it conceives of the pursuit of health.